SMALL BUSINESS PROMOTION
Case Studies from Developing Countries

SMALL BUSINESS PROMOTION

Case Studies from Developing Countries

MALCOLM HARPER and
KAVIL RAMACHANDRAN

INTERMEDIATE TECHNOLOGY PUBLICATIONS   1984

Published by ITDG Publishing
103–105 Southampton Row, London WC1B 4HL, UK
www.itdgpublishing.org.uk

© Intermediate Technology Publications 1984

First published in 1984
Print on demand since 2003

ISBN 0 946688 45 1

A catalogue record for this book is available from the British Library

ITDG Publishing is the publishing arm of the Intermediate Technology
Development Group. Our mission is to build the skills and capacity
of people in developing countries through the dissemination of
information in all forms, enabling them to improve the quality
of their lives and that of future generations.

Typeset by Inforum Ltd, Portsmouth
Printed in Great Britain by Lightning Source, Milton Keynes

CONTENTS

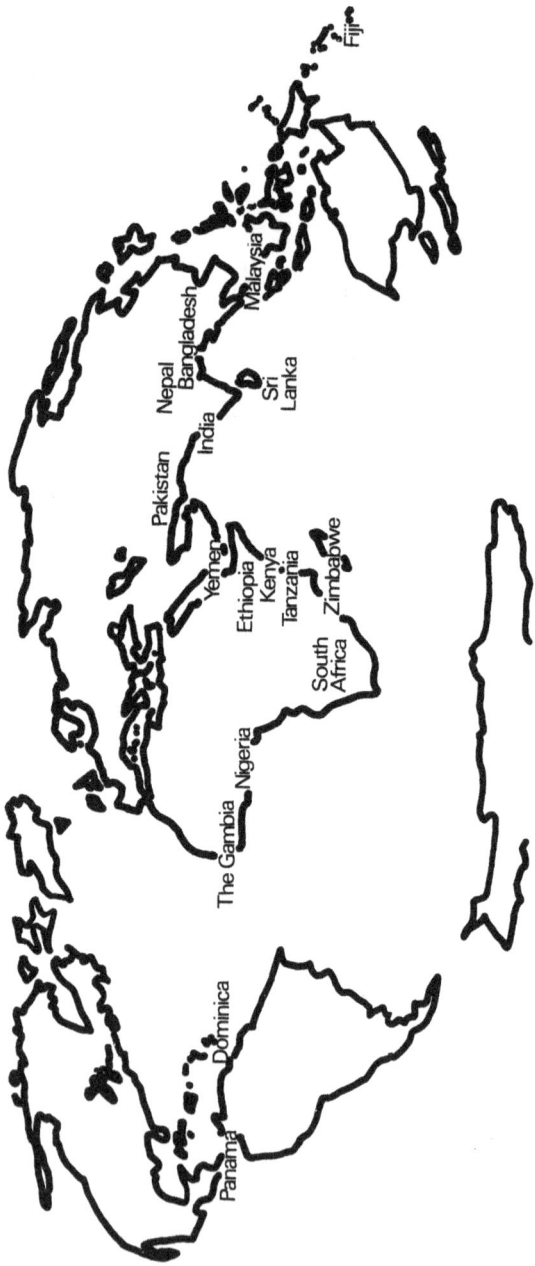

Fiji

Malaysia

Nepal
Bangladesh

Pakistan

India

Sri
Lanka

Yemen

Ethiopia
Kenya
Tanzania

Zimbabwe

South
Africa

Nigeria

The Gambia

Dominica

Panama

INTRODUCTION

Twenty-two of these case studies were written by participants in the annual Cranfield programme on the Promotion of Small-Scale Enterprises in Developing Countries, between 1978 and 1983, while the remaining six were contributed to a collection of material on industrial co-operatives, sponsored by the MATCOM (Material and Techniques for Co-operative Management Training) Project of the International Labour Office. All the writers were personally familiar with the enterprises they have described, and in most cases they were closely involved with them as representatives of banks or other assistance agencies. The names of the businesses, and their exact locations, have in some cases been disguised, and the financial information has been simplified and converted approximately into United States dollars. Apart from some editing, the cases are otherwise exactly as they were written.

The studies were originally prepared for use in the Cranfield training programme and other courses for people working with small enterprises in developing countries, in order to ensure that discussions related to real life situations and to enterprises with which the participants were actively involved. The conclusions reached during the discussion sessions, which are in most cases very briefly summarized in the comments which follow each case, were not only interesting for all the participants but were of practical value, and were then possibly implemented by the writers when they returned to their jobs.

These case studies were very valuable when used in this way, and they more than justified the effort which had been put into writing them. We felt, however, that they deserved a wider circulation. There are large numbers of surveys and research papers about small enterprises, and more are published every year. Very often, however, they consist only of generalized statistics about the origins of the entrepreneurs, the profitability of large numbers of enterprises, their use of various types of technology, the repayment results of credit programmes and so on. This data is valuable, and is in fact an essential basis for understanding the economic role and problems of small enterprises in developing countries, and for designing programmes and framing policies to assist them. There is sometimes a need, however, for flesh on the statistical bones. We do not for a moment suggest that these case studies are drawn from a random or representative sample of small enterprises in developing countries, but they do describe typical situations in a simple way, which may be particularly useful for people who have had little opportunity actually to work in close contact with entrepreneurs for very extended periods.

Some two thirds of the case studies describe what might be called failures. A proportion of small enterprises do in fact fail, and this is one reason why the sector as a whole remains dynamic and is able to respond so quickly to changing circumstances. The predominance of failure in this collection is therefore not unrepresentative of reality, but the reader should not conclude that the vast majority of enterprises fail, or that any attempts to assist them are bound to make things worse. The participants in the Cranfield programme were asked to prepare descriptions of enterprises with which they were personally involved, and which would raise issues of interest to their colleagues on the programme. Since they all worked for enterprise assistance agencies, they were more likely to be familiar with businesses in need of assistance. It should be evident, however, that many of the problems have arisen because of well-meaning official attempts to help. One objective of this publication is to show how this can happen.

About half these studies concern co-operatives. In fact, of course co-operative enterprises make up only a tiny proportion of small businesses in developing countries, or anywhere else. They are over-represented in this collection, however, because they do receive a disproportionate amount of attention from local and international assistance agencies. There are numerous reasons for this: co-operatives are often politically acceptable when individual enterprise is not, and they are believed to be more equitable than private businesses and more effective than Government controlled ones. They are also very difficult to manage and may be totally inappropriate to the circumstances in which they are introduced. The twelve examples in this collection may alert readers to some of the dangers in this field, and illustrate some of the conditions which appear likely to lead to success.

The case studies are drawn from 17 different countries, in every continent, and they include familiar non-farming activities such as garment manufacture and handicrafts, or vehicle repair, together with more unusual businesses such as sculpture, aluminium hollow ware and a steel rolling mill. It is impossible to classify them in any meaningful way, and it did not seem appropriate to try to put them into categories according to the type of problem which appeared most important. They exemplify, indeed, both the diversity of small enterprise activities and problems, and the impossibility of trying to concentrate on one particular aspect without considering the business as a whole. The owner or manager of a small enterprise must be a generalist, and he cannot consider marketing, finance, technology or anything else in isolation. The same applies to those working with small enterprises. They may eventually identify particular problems which require particular attention, but they must initially look at the business as a whole.

The comments which follow each case study are necessarily brief, and may be thought to be excessively contentious. They do generally summarize, however, the consensus of the participants in the Cranfield programme, in so far as any consensus could be reached as a result of one hour or two of discussion. They tend to represent a non-interventionist point of view, which may have originated in part from the prejudices of the discussion leader but were also based on the bitter experience of participants. The comments do not, of course, give all the alternative explanations which might be suggested for the situations described, nor do they include a full range of alternative solutions to every problem that has been diagnosed.

It would be perfectly possible, and legitimate, to put foward totally different suggestions. Some may argue that more rather than less Government and international protection and assistance is needed to redress the imbalance between large and small enterprises, or between rich and poor countries. Others may suggest that the whole structure of society is unjust – small enterprises, and less developed countries themselves, are bound to continue to be exploited and to remain on the periphery of development. The difficulties described in these case studies, some would argue, could only be remedied by a revolution. The views expressed in the comments on each case study may be a convenient foil, which people with contrary opinions can use to strengthen their own conviction that they are nearer to the truth.

It would certainly be most unfortunate if any instructor who wished to use a case study as a basis for discussion was to direct his students towards the conclusions suggested in the comment, or to suggest that this is the right answer. One great merit of case studies is that they demonstrate that it is more important, and more difficult, to identify the problems than to find solutions, and that there are no right or wrong answers to genuine management problems.

Case studies of this sort have been used successfully with groups of senior academics, civil servants or bankers, with secondary school pupils, and with people of every degree of seniority and experience in between. The level of discussion is obviously different for each group, depending on their learning objective. The simple accounts which are available in some of the studies can be used as a basis for instruction in simple financial analysis and management. The problems faced by the entrepreneurs provide simple but sometimes very profound lessons in management, which are as applicable to large-scale businesses as to small ones. The impact of Government programmes on the businesses can be used in seminars for planners and policy makers, both as examples of what has happened and as a basis for the hypothetical question, 'How would this entrepreneur be likely to respond to this type of policy or other intervention we are considering?'.

Some readers may feel that the cases are too brief or quite irrelevant to the particular circumstances with which they themselves are faced. They may be correct; this collection will have been enormously valuable if such readers throw this book away and visit some small business people in their own communities, in order to produce similar material which is locally relevant. Entrepreneurs are usually very willing to talk freely to anyone who shows a geniune interest in their problems. People who think that they will find it difficult to obtain access to the businesses, and that their owners will be reluctant to talk to them, have often found that their main difficulty is to get away from the owner of the business who so appreciates the opportunity to talk about what he or she is doing. The resulting case studies can, if necessary, easily be disguised, since there are so many similar small businesses in most communities, and the necessary inquiries and writing can be completed quite quickly and easily. Anyone who is conducting courses for people who train, advise or lend money to small enterprises, or for small business people themselves, should seriously consider asking participants to prepare simple case studies such as those in this collection, which can then be used as training material in the course itself.

Small enterprises have always had problems, and a similar collection of case studies written in 1977 suggests that these problems have not changed very much. Many of those who assist small businesses, however, have to some extent modified their approach. It has become clear that official programmes cannot achieve a great deal, unless the policy environment is favourable. Even then, they can claim no more than a catalytic role. It is even more important that the individual with whom they are dealing should possess the necessary entrepreneurial qualities. Academics and practitioners are intensifying their search for techniques to identify such people before they start a business, or to reveal or increase entrepreneurship among groups who are not presently playing their proper part in the economy.

There is also an increasing realization that the potential and problems of small enterprises in the so-called developing countries are not very different from those in the rich, developed and industrialized parts of the world. Underprivileged groups in decayed inner cities or backward rural areas of Europe or North America need the same sort of encouragement and assistance to enterprise as similar people in Africa, Asia or Latin America, and some of the experience of promoting small enterprise in poor countries is now being applied in rich ones. This book aims to convey some impression of what small enterprises are like. We hope that it will encourage readers, in any country, to find out more for themselves in their own community, so that they can buy from them, sell to them, finance, assist, advise or train them – or actually themselves start and manage a small business more successfully.

Malcolm Harper and
Kavil Ramachandran,
Cranfield,
February 1984

THE AL-ROADHAH WEAVERS CO-OPERATIVE, SOUTH YEMEN

Al-Roadhah is a small town in the People's Democratic Republic of The Yemen, about 350 kilometres away from the capital city of Aden. Al-Roadhah has, since time immemorial, been a traditional centre for weavers; nobody knows when the trade started in the town, but the shawls that are made there are very similar to those which were sold in the ancient markets of Mesopotamia, Persia and the Mediterranean Basin more than 2,000 years ago.

The Yemen has for centuries been a centre for a number of different handicrafts, but many of them only survive in examples that are exhibited at the National Museums. In recent years, as modern mass-produced products have come to dominate world markets, many of the traditional Yemeni handicraft industries have disappeared because they could not compete with imported commodities. Even those skills that have not disappeared altogether have in many cases seriously deteriorated.

In an attempt to remedy this situation, the Revolutionary Government has, since independence in 1967, attempted to preserve and promote those handicraft industries that still exist, as a part of the national culture of the country. It has tried to help them use local raw materials and produce products which would help to meet the needs of society.

This policy has been supported at the highest level and in 1971 a special decree was issued to allow the leather handicraft workers of Aden to form a co-operative for themselves. From then on the concept of handicraft co-operatives was extended to different types of handicrafts, throughout the country, and by 1975 nine co-operatives had been formed.

One of these is the Al-Roadhah Weavers Co-operative. In 1974, 44 weavers from the town agreed to form a Society, and their Co-operative was formally registered by the State Department of Co-operatives in September of that year. The 44 men who started the Society had all been weavers for many years and were part of the large family of weavers in the town. Their aim was to ensure a regular and resonably priced supply of raw materials, to improve the marketing of their products and to better their working conditions by improving the methods of manufacture. They also hoped to promote employment, and to preserve their craft, by attracting young people to the trade.

They selected a young man who was the son of one of the original members to be the Manager of the Society. He was an intelligent young man who had graduated from secondary school and had taken a special three months' training course in management and accountancy at the National Co-operative Training Institute. The son of one of the other founder members, who had also been trained at the Institute, was recruited as Accountant to keep the books for the Society.

At the beginning the members contributed a total of $300 share capital, and the Government arranged an overdraft for them at the National Bank of Yemen, free of interest, to enable the new Co-operative to finance its activities. Its first operation was to obtain raw materials for the members, so that they could weave the traditional men's kilts which were their main item of production.

In spite of their best efforts, the members and their Manager found it difficult to obtain regular supplies of good quality raw materials. This meant that their members could maintain neither the volume nor the quality of their production, and they failed to compete with individual weavers who seemed to be able to obtain raw materials through channels of their own. As a result the Co-operative failed to sell its members' products, and during 1978 the situation was so serious that only 40% of what they made could be sold. A number of the younger members left the Society in order to take jobs on construction sites, and the Society had reached a serious crisis in its affairs.

At the end of 1978 the members decided that they should make a determined attempt to improve the quality and variety of the raw materials they were buying, and they decided to encourage women who were without any means of earning an income to join and work in the Co-operative. By this time the Ministry of Industry had taken over the supervision of handicraft co-operatives from the Ministry of Agriculture, and they helped the Society to obtain an import licence in order to purchase raw materials from Japan. They also arranged for the Society's overdraft facility to be increased to $90,000. In order to encourage women to join, the Society constructed a new hall for them; the local authorities helped by providing some building materials, but all the work was carried out by local people from the town on a voluntary basis.

An elderly weaver, who had already volunteered to train some of the younger members, was now employed full time by the Co-operative as Training Officer and Production Manager. He trained 45 women weavers, who formed a totally new production unit in the Society. He also designed a modified hand-loom which enabled people to produce more cloth in the same time, and by 1983 a total of 155 women had joined the Society.

During the five years since they adopted their new policy, the Society's production has increased both in quantity and quality. They no longer have problems in importing raw materials, and are also able to supply raw materials to non-members in the area at reasonable prices. They have opened shops in Aden and in Mukalla, the second city in Yemen, in order to display and sell their products direct to customers. Production went up by two and a half times between 1978 and 1981, and sales increased from $30,000 per year to $300,000 per year over the same period.

As a result of their success the Society has been able to earn a considerable surplus and to pay very fair wages to its members. They are paid on the basis of what they produce, and women earn around $150 a month while men can earn as much as $300. Men and women are paid the same amount per piece, but the women earn less because they have to spend a proportion of their time on housework.

In order to strengthen its finances and increase its activities the Society has reinvested its surplus in its own operations, and by the end of 1981 they had reinvested a total of $450,000 in this way. Membership had reached a total of 221 people, and the Society had become a major force in the community.

In addition to providing so many people with a reasonable livelihood, the Society launched a literacy programme among its members, and by 1980 all the members were able to read and write; when they joined, all the women had been illiterate. Early in 1981 the Society started a further education class for those who wished to join, and 33 members joined, 31 of whom were women; 28 of them sat the examination for the primary school education certificate and passed successfully. Officials from the Co-operative Training Institute in Aden visit Al-Roadhah from time to time and run training programmes and show films to the members. In addition, the Society bought a film projector in 1981 and a video recorder in the following year, since it is impossible to receive television programmes in Al-Roadhah.

Comment

This is an unusual and encouraging example of a successful Co-operative, in a country which has a strong ideological commitment to State and community enterprise. In contrast to other similar ventures elsewhere, it is significant that Government merely provided the legislative framework within which individual craftsmen could come together and start co-operative societies. The Society was not 'promoted' by a zealous Co-operative Officer, but was the result of its founder members' initiative.

The members all shared similar skills, and they were fortunate enough to identify talented Managers who were also from the same community. Problems have often arisen when relatives are appointed in this way; the social cohesion of the weaving community in this remote town seems to have been such that younger educated people were not tempted to misuse their position. The Society was vigorously supported by the local community, who were willing to contribute their labour without cost for special projects. The whole enterprise appears to be based on the desire of the community to benefit from progress without destroying its traditional crafts and social unity.

Government has provided modest assistance, such as the interest free loan and training services, but has not in any way attempted to take over the operations of the Society. In 1978, when the Society was faced with a serious crisis, the members themselves had to decide what to do. The Government was able to help them with import licences, but this was in response to members' appreciation of the gravity of their problems, and their determination to do everything they could to solve them themselves. The Society is now satisfying the community's need for higher incomes, and is also providing education, training and even entertainment. It demonstrates that co-operatives can achieve success, so long as they are the result of local initiative and are not smothered with excessive Government assistance.

THE BHAKTAPUR WOMEN'S TAILORING CO-OPERATIVE, NEPAL

Bhaktapur is a town of around 150,000 people, situated in the Kathmandu Valley about 25 kilometres west of the capital city of the Kingdom of Nepal. The town has largely been by-passed by the development that has taken place in the Valley, and there is a desperate need to create new sources of income for the rapidly growing but seriously impoverished population.

The Bhaktapur Women's Tailoring Co-operative was started in the town in 1979. The Society was the brain-child of the local Branch Manager of the Industrial Services Centre, a national industrial promotion institution which had an office in the town. He encouraged a local entrepreneur, who was at that time running her own private tailoring school, to form about 30 of her trainees into a co-operative. He prepared a feasibility study for them and suggested that they should approach the local branch of the Agricultural Development Bank for an unsecured loan at the subsidized interest rate of 6% per year.

They asked for a loan of $8,000, including $2,000 for sewing machines and $6,000 for working capital. The women themselves raised a further $1,800 in share capital. This Bank had previously operated as the Co-operative Bank of Nepal and its staff were thus very anxious to grant a loan to what was at that time only the second industrial co-operative in the Kingdom. The loan was appraised and approved in just two weeks, and the Bank's staff had little opportunity to examine in any detail the figures that were presented.

In order to ensure that the Bank and the other supporting institutions such as the Industrial Services Centre would be fully committed to the venture in the long term, the members, who were mainly from middle class backgrounds, together with the Branch Manager, succeeded in persuading the Prime Minister of the country to preside over the ceremonial opening of the Society.

The ceremony was a great success; for the first and perhaps the only time in the history of the Society all the members were present. For them the Prime Minister's presence at the opening represented the culmination of two months' work of preparing the study, registering the Society, obtaining a bank loan and organizing the actual opening feast. The members were at this time very enthusiastic and totally committed to the Society and its future. Later, when they were faced with the actual tasks of operating commercially and competing with other private manufacturers, their enthusiasm tended to decline.

Shortly after the Society started, the Branch Manager of the Industrial Services Centre, who had been its keenest supporter, was removed from his post for political reasons. Just before he left he asked a German aid financed urban development project, the Bhaktapur Development Project, to take the new Society under its wing and to do whatever was possible to assist the women in their new venture. In response to this request the wife of one of the German Project's foreign staff started to give regular lessons in basic accounting to the two members of the Society who acted as its managers. They did their best, but since they had no background in commercial affairs they were not able to apply very much of what they learnt.

The Society started production using the working capital they had borrowed from the Bank. The woman who had previously run the private training school, and who was acting as Manager, recommended that they should make pyjamas and her suggestion was accepted. She came to this conclusion after surveying the market and observing that fine cotton pyjamas from China were selling very well. The members agreed with her that if the Chinese could sell pyjamas for $7 a pair in Nepal, a local producer would certainly be able to make and sell them for less.

Since this was their first production run the women enthusiastically set about producing 100 sets of pyjamas of various sizes. They found, however, when they had finished the order that, because their products were of an inferior quality to the Chinese pyjamas, not a single pair could be sold without drastically reducing the price. They were, however, very reluctant to do this since they were so proud of the goods they had succeeded in producing.

Various members of the German group in the town took some interest in the new Society, and when they heard about the problem they helped the members to calculate how much it had actually cost them to make the pyjamas. They discovered that the real cost was some 25% higher than their original estimate of the selling price, and as a result the had over $700 worth of dead stock. Although a number of people, including the Bank Manager, advised the women to think very carefully before making anything else, they continued to produce further items on the same basis and after about a year they had some $2,000 worth of dead stock. During this whole period their major emphasis was on productive employment for themselves rather than on sales or profits.

The women still had not used up all the money they had received as a loan for working capital, and they succeeded in obtaining two orders from charitable organizations which were attracted by the fact that all the tailors were women, and were organized as a co-operative. At this point their monthly sales were around $250, whereas they had estimated in their original study that they would achieve a figure of $2,500 per month. They had also calculated that the break even point would be $1,250 per month. They had allowed for a rather high level of salaries, particularly for the two Managers, which they calculated would absorb over two-thirds of their sales revenue altogether.

Six months had now gone by since the Society had started and the women realized that they had to increase their sales. They decided to appeal to the German Project for a marketing adviser for a period of three months. The Project had by this time set up a special programme to assist local enterprise and they agreed, with some prompting from the Bank and the National Registrar of Co-operatives, to pay for a German marketing expert to be attached to the Society for a period of three months; this was later extended by a further month.

The adviser investigated the situation of the Society fairly deeply, and found that marketing was only one of their problems. Their other difficulties included low quality, high costs because of the excessive salaries and other fixed costs, unreliable deliveries, differences in colours and cloth between order specifications and what they finally produced, and the low motivation and poor attendance record of the worker members. Generally speaking, their problems arose from bad management.

Nevertheless, the adviser worked very hard and was able to help the Society to increase its turnover from $250 to $1,000 per month. This was still below the break even point but was a great improvement. The adviser guided the management on how to obtain orders, how and when to give discounts, what products to produce and on almost every aspect of business management. The Germans even went so far as to bring in the National Co-operative Training Institute to provide a special one week course to the whole group on co-operative management.

The adviser surveyed the local market in some detail and concluded that because of poor management, high costs and a number of other factors it would be impossible for the Society to sell its goods locally in competition with local producers who had studied the market more closely and paid their workers very low wages. In any case, the local people had very little money to spend.

Foreign importers, on the other hand, would be likely to favour the Society because it was a women's organization, it was a co-operative and its products came from the remote and romantic Himalayas. The future seemed brighter as export orders continued to come in as a result of the expert's efforts, and the women asked the Germans to provide somebody else to look after quality control. Again they agreed, and they paid a Swiss lady who had been a seamstress to work with the Society for five half days a week for a year. During its first year the Society lost something under $1,000; during the second year the loss was reduced to around $250 and although this was an improvement the Society still had a long way to go before it could be called a genuinely viable operation.

In spite of their improved quality, the Society was still unable to meet delivery dates. This was partly because the management had by this time become used to being told what to do by the foreign advisers, and they lacked any individual initiative themselves. They found it difficult to obtain the cloth they required for the orders, they had to make last minute design changes without agreeing with their customers, they failed to obtain export licences on time and they had to rely on their friends among the German Project and others to transport the goods to Europe. In spite of the efforts of the adviser the export orders gradually fell away, production dropped and members ceased to come to the workshop because there was no work for them.

After two and a half years of losses it was clear that there had to be a change in management. One of the Managers left to go into politics and the other returned to the University to take a Masters Degree in education. There was a good deal of disagreement among

The Bhaktapur Women's Tailoring Co-operative
Balance Sheets as at 31 December 1980 and 1981

Liabilities	December 1981 $	December 1980 $
Share Capital	1,300	1,300
Less: Accumulated Losses	1,220	970
Net Members' Capital	80	330
Loan from Bank	4,500	4,000
Accounts Payable	290	550
Customer Deposit	120	120
Total Liabilities	$4,990	$5,000

Assets	$	$
Cash and Bank Balance	130	750
Stocks	2,870	2,070
Furniture and Equipment	1,740	1,930
Other Assets	250	250
Total Assets	$4,990	$5,000

the members after the Managers left, and they eventually selected a kind but somewhat ineffectual Manager from amongst their own numbers. At this point the Society almost ceased to exist, and there was only enough work for one or two of the members on a part-time basis.

The Bank was still trying to recover its money by reviving the Society, and they offered a local private exporter the chance of managing the Society. Although it appeared on the face of it to be a thankless task, she seriously considered the opportunity because she lacked security for a loan to finance her own garment exports which were doing reasonably well at the time. She realized that the Bank would be willing to extend further credit to the Society if it was under her management, and she thought that she would then be able to use the Society's working capital to finance her own business and also to export garments made by the Society through her own contacts.

Comment

This Society was promoted by an outsider, who apparently had the best of intentions, but it was not in response to his need for employment, nor did his career depend on its success. The women who joined, and in particular the entrepreneur who was persuaded to be the Manager, were able to be persuaded to become involved but the Society was not an expression of their own felt need, nor was it based on any existing association.

At the beginning the members, and the various supporting institutions, may to some extent have been deluded by the general air of enthusiasm and support for the venture. Co-operative ventures, and income generating activities for women are fashionable in development circles, and they were even able to persuade the Prime Minister himself to be present at the feast which celebrated the opening of the Society. To many people, and perhaps to the members themselves at this stage, the opening of the Society became an end in itself; they forgot that its purpose was to generate income and to become a viable enterprise.

The initiator of the Society may not have been a member himself, but he was entrepreneurial enough to have the idea and to push it forward. His unexpected departure illustrates the danger of reliance on outsiders, who may for reasons quite beyond their control have to desert the infant enterprises they have helped to start.

After his departure, the Society came increasingly to rely on part-time foreign advisers. These may well have been people of great talent and experience, who were totally committed to their work, but their intervention was necessarily on a short term and advisory basis. To make good use of consultants or advisers is one of the most difficult things a manager has to do. It was quite unreasonable to expect the inexperienced women who were responsible for the Society's affairs to use these outsiders as advisers, and they inevitably allowed them to become the actual managers. This may have been reasonable in the short term, but the Society rapidly became wholly dependent on outside advisers, and its own Managers became even less capable of taking over the affairs of the Society on the departure of the foreigners. In spite, or perhaps because of, the large amount of assistance they had received, the Society was totally unviable two years after it had started.

The Manager of the Bank is probably correct to look for an outside entrepreneur to take over the Society, both because this may lead to the recovery of his loan and because it is one way in which the employment objectives of the enterprise may still be achieved. If the entrepreneur is able to obtain a loan through her position in the Society, this will achieve her own objectives and also the aims for which the Society was originally established. It is impossible to force co-operative enterprise to take root in a society where it will not flourish naturally, and any attempt artificially to prolong the life of the Co-operative Society without the involvement of private entrepreneurs is likely to lead to further losses without creating viable long term employment for the women of Bhaktapur.

BONALIM SWEETS LIMITED, BANGLADESH

Mr. Rahman obtained a Master of Commerce Degree from Dacca University in 1961. He considered various types of employment, and eventually took a job with the Bangladesh Small and Cottage Industries Corporation in 1963 as a junior officer. In 1966 he married the daughter of an industrialist. His father-in-law had interests in many fields, and in 1974 Mr. Rahman was able through his position in the Bangladesh Small and Cottage Industries Corporation to help him to set up a biscuit making plant, using West German machinery.

At that period the Government of Bangladesh operated a system whereby basic food stuffs such as flour, sugar, soya bean and vegetable oil, which were very expensive in the open market, were made available at a very much reduced price to certain industrial units which had been set up with the Government's blessing. This scheme was designed to encourage the development of a local industrial base and Mr. Rahman was able to obtain this special privilege for his father-in-law's enterprise. As a result the business prospered since its costs were much lower than many of its competitors who did not enjoy the privileged access to low priced raw materials. The business grew rapidly and in 1975 Mr. Rahman resigned from the Corporation and joined the management of his father-in-law's business.

As a result of his experience with his father-in-law Mr. Rahman then decided to start his own business. He had by this time gained a little familiarity with food manufacturing, and he wanted to find a business where the low priced raw materials would be particularly advantageous. He therefore selected confectionery manufacturing, and made a visit to West Germany and the United Kingdom to select the special modern machinery which was needed to make sweets of the highest quality. In 1979 he finalized his arrangements and the Government gave him permission to import the machinery and to obtain sugar at the special privileged price.

Bonalim Sweets started operations towards the end of 1979. The machinery was mainly automatic and cost a total of $65,000; a further $35,000 was invested in land and buildings. The Government had allocated foreign exchange to Mr. Rahman for the purchase of his equipment on the condition that 50% of the business's production would be exported. They agreed to provide import licences for subsequent purchases of foreign raw materials so long as the export performance came up to expectations.

The business ran successfully for the first two years and although Mr. Rahman did not succeed in actually exporting any of its products he was able to continue obtaining foreign exchange to purchase raw material, and to buy sugar at the reduced price, since he claimed that it took time to develop export markets. It was in fact very easy to sell the company's products on the local market since sugar was by far the most important raw material and very few other manufacturers were able to buy it at such a low price. Some companies which enjoyed this privilege did not bother to use the sugar but merely sold it at a profit; Mr. Rahman did not choose to do this, but used the sugar to manufacture confectionery which he sold at a large profit.

At the beginning of 1981 the Government refused to issue any further import licences to Bonalim Sweets, since no export sales had been made. Towards the end of the same year the Government also stopped the scheme whereby certain companies were able to buy raw materials at low prices, and from then on all companies had to buy at the same price as everybody else. These two changes were naturally a very serious blow to Bonalim Sweets; its profits disappeared, production fell and the company had to face genuine competition for the first time.

In order to attempt to secure the renewal of their import licences the company approached the Bangladesh Export Promotion Bureau for advice on obtaining export orders. The Bureau claimed that there was export potential for the company's products in the Middle East and elsewhere but Mr. Rahman was not actually able to obtain any orders. They also started to lose ground in the home market. Other firms with simpler machinery and lower capital investment were able to offer their products at cheaper prices now that Bonalim Sweets no longer had access to low cost raw materials.

Bonalim Sweets reacted to the competition in the domestic market by considering the manufacture of cheaper and lower quality products. It had not up to this time found it necessary to organize its marketing in a particularly aggressive way; all its customers had to pay cash, and the company would only deliver goods within the Dacca city area. It would only accept orders from other parts of the country if the customers paid cash in advance, and the company had no agents or dealers and refused to offer credit facilities to anyone.

Mr. Rahman's father-in-law's biscuit factory also suffered from the same problems as Bonalim Sweets, and as a result actually had to close down. By this time Mr. Rahman's brother-in-law had joined his father in the biscuit factory, and was vigorously trying to re-establish the business on the basis of the new situation which it faced. He also wanted to help Bonalim Sweets, and Mr. Rahman was glad of his assistance. They found the situation of both companies very difficult, however, since both had been set up with largely automatic imported machinery and were dependent on imported materials and on the special price privilege which they had previously enjoyed.

Comment

The Government policy, which was designed to promote local industry, has in fact promoted industries that are capital rather than labour intensive and are also dependent on imported materials. The Government's policy has thus encouraged people to set up businesses which dramatically fail to share two of the major advantages of small enterprises, that is labour intensity and the use of local raw materials.

In addition, the businesses have been established on the basis of their access to special low priced raw materials. This privilege is not provided as a reward for export success, but purely on the basis of expectations of future potential. This misguided pricing policy enabled businesses which used foreign equipment, rather than local labour, to under-cut the prices of smaller more labour intensive local industries and thus to defeat many of the objectives of development.

It is hardly surprising, in the circumstances, that the Bonalim Sweets company found it hard to cope with the new situation it faced when the Government corrected its policies. There had been no need for a proper marketing organization, and it had proved possible for two years to continue to obtain foreign exchange without having to incur the expense and effort involved in actually obtaining export orders. Both businesses, in fact, were totally dependent on the Government subsidies which were not in the interests of society as a whole.

Mr. Rahman and his father-in-law can scarcely be blamed for establishing their enterprises on the basis of Government policies that were in force at the time they started. It may prove difficult, if not impossible, to restructure the enterprises so that they will be able to compete in a new situation. There is no reason, however, why Government should provide any special assistance in order to prolong the life of enterprises which are fundamentally uneconomic. The investors have presumably made good profits in previous years, and if they can use these to revive their enterprises by making them more in tune with economic realities, this will be all to the good. If not, however, it may be in the best interests of society for the factories to remain closed, so that the demand for their products can be satisfied by other smaller enterprises which employ more labour and use fewer imported materials.

THE CANON PATERSON CRAFT CENTRE CO-OPERATIVE, ZIMBABWE

Canon Paterson was an Anglican clergyman who had for many years organized small groups of sculptors in different parts of what was then Rhodesia. The aim of these welfare groups, as they were then called, was to teach young school leavers, who had had very little education, how to be sculptors in order to give them an opportunity to earn a living. He organized many of these groups, wherever he happened to be posted, and the last group he set up was in Harare, in the centre of the then city of Salisbury.

Canon Paterson had succeeded in keeping these groups going through his own personal initiative and energy; when he suddenly died early in 1974, the Harare group was leaderless. The group would undoubtedly have collapsed, but somebody advised them to form a co-operative society so that they could qualify for assistance from Government and other sources. The members got together, subscribed $2 each as initial capital and applied to the City Council for premises. They were allowed to use a building which was ideal for their purposes, with running water, electricity and telephone, and they only had to pay a nominal rent for it. They had around 50 members at the time. They elected a Committee of seven members, from whom they selected a Chairman, Vice Chairman, Secretary and Assistant Secretary. The age of the members ranged from 16 to 41 years old.

The main function of the Society is to assist its members to obtain raw material and to market their carvings. The Society buys about 40 tons of stone a month from quarries some 200 kilometres away from the city and ships this to its premises. It adds on a margin to cover the costs of transport and other handling charges, and the stone is then sold to members in the small quantities they require. Non-members can also buy stone, at a slightly higher price.

The members make the carvings on their own, and they produce a wide range of different articles. They can if they wish sell their carvings through the Society's premises, in which case they have to pay a 5% commission to cover expenses. They can also sell their carvings independently, and as a result it is difficult to know how good a living they are making. It appears that most of them, however, do make use of the Society's premises since they are very well situated in the centre of the city and can attract large numbers of buyers fairly easily.

Every member has to pay a monthly subscription of $2.75 to cover regular expenses such as rent, telephone and water, and these subscriptions, along with the small margin on the stone and the sales commission represent the main income of the Society.

Until 1980 the Society did very well without any assistance from Government or other external sources, apart from the subsidized premises. It accumulated a total of $9,000 from its earnings, and membership rose to over 120 at one stage in 1979. The Chairman and the Vice Chairman had occupied their positions for some years, and were generally respected by the members. The Chairman was only 31 years old, but had had two years of secondary education; his Vice Chairman was ten years older, but had only been to primary school.

There was a hard core of long-standing members, like the Chairman and Vice Chairman, but there was a high turnover among the younger members. Many of them thought that sculpture was an easy way of earning a living. They would join the Society, buy some stone and soon find out that there was more to it than they thought. They would lose interest and it was often difficult to collect subscriptions from them. In addition, some of the older members sometimes found it difficult to sell their sculptures. In these cases they would often refuse to pay their subscriptions, and the Committee found it necessary to debar the premises to anyone who was not paid up to date. This caused a certain amount of ill-will.

Rhodesia gained its independence in 1980, and became Zimbabwe. The non-African community who had been the main purchasers of sculpture started to leave the country in large numbers, and fewer tourists visited from South Africa. The guerilla activities in many parts of the country also created problems, and as a result the Society started to experience serious difficulties. It maintained its business through 1980, and earned an increased surplus of $5,000 in that year, but the surplus fell to $3,200 in 1981 and the Society's working capital position began to give cause for concern.

In addition to declining demand, the price of raw materials and other overheads was rising with general inflation, and large numbers of unsold carvings started to accumulate in the Society's workshop. Membership fell to under 60 people and, although a number of them continued to use the workshop as a social centre, fewer and fewer of the members were actually engaged in sculpture.

Because of these problems, the Committee decided in 1981 to seek outside assistance for the first time. Until then there had been no need for additional finance or technical assistance, but the Committee members made inquiries and eventually identified a voluntary agency which was willing to help them. They received a grant of $5,000, and the Ministry of Commerce, which is responsible for co-operative affairs, helped them to display some of their sculptures at an exhibition in West Germany. This was not successful, since there was nobody to take care of the carvings; a number of them were broken and only a few were sold. The officials responsible for the exhibition reported that most customers in Germany had commented on the poor quality of the carvings; they would have to improve if they wanted to capture export markets.

Local sales proved no easier; the new African elite that had replaced the colonialists had little or no interest in local sculpture, and attempts to sell the members' products at shows in different parts of the country met with little success. It was suggested that they should open a new showroom in the centre of Harare but it was not clear how they would obtain premises, or who would manage it. Because of the shortage of funds, the Society fell behind in its payments for stone. As a result, the quarry owner demanded cash for all future consignments, and this made it difficult for the Society to obtain even the limited amount of stone which its members now required.

In desperation, the Chairman called on the Minister of Commerce himself and asked him and the officials responsible for co-operative affairs to help them to find new export markets for their members' products. The Minister promised that he would help, but in spite of repeated requests all that the Chairman was able to obtain was assurances that 'something was being done about the matter'. A small number of members continued to produce a few sculptures, for sale to some of Zimbabwe's remaining foreign residents, and one of the Government officials at the Ministry told the members that the world economy was picking up. He assured them that business would soon start to come in, as tourists arrived from Western Europe, America and so on. Most of the members were very sceptical, and continued their search for other ways of earning a living.

Comment

At the beginning, this Society enjoyed many of the conditions which are generally conducive to the success of co-operative enterprise. The group had been established by one of those rare people who are prepared to contribute their energy and commitment to a group from which they will gain no particular financial benefit. When the founder died, the members were faced with a sudden and acute crisis. If they did nothing, they would lose their livelihood; as a result they formed the Society and proceeded to manage it successfully.

The Society flourished for some years, in spite, or perhaps

because, of having received very little external assistance. It accumulated a relatively large amount of money, from a very small capital base, and it appears to have been properly directed and to have satisfactorily catered to its members' need for raw material and display facilities.

Political independence, as so often is the case, radically changed the market. Local people had little interest in traditional sculpture, and members were unable to respond to the changed circumstances. Export sales are generally more difficult than sales to local expatriates or tourists, and it was therefore not surprising that the first disorganized attempt at exporting was a failure.

Government advisers, as is all too often the case, did not have the courage to tell the Society the truth about the situation. They put the members off with promises which could never be fulfilled, and provided further excuses for the members to avoid facing the facts as they really were. Dishonest assurances of this sort are actually not in the interests of any co-operative society, or other small enterprise, since people are far more likely to respond positively to a sudden shock than to a gradual decline in their business. The members' original response to Canon Paterson's death demonstrated that co-operatives, like individuals or whole countries, can often build success on the basis of apparent disaster. Grants of money, or empty promises, will only prolong the agony. The members must not be protected from reality, and it may be that they will respond as positively as they did in 1974 when the Society was originally formed.

Women members of the Al-Roadah Weavers' Co-operative (the first case study).

A solitary tailor in Nepal (– a contrast to co-operative work).

A sewing co-operative.

THE DRUM MANUFACTURING COMPANY, INDIA

Mr. Shah was a Production Supervisor in a sheet metal fabrication factory in a large town in northern India. He had observed that the chemical industry was growing in the town, and that a number of other businesses were locating storage warehouses in the area, since it was centrally situated for communications with the rest of the country.

Many of these businesses made extensive use of steel drums and other containers for storage purposes. Some of them had approached Mr. Shah's employers to see if they could buy items of this sort from them, but the Company's capacity was largely devoted to the manufacture of steel shelving and similar products, and its management had no interest in expanding into the manufacture of storage drums.

Mr. Shah had accummulated a certain amount of savings over the years, and decided to set up his own business to satisfy this demand. He started in 1970 in a small workshop on the edge of the city with a capital investment of $1,500; he only used very rudimentary equipment and employed three skilled and two semi-skilled workers to manufacture his products. For its first two years the business was very profitable and Mr. Shah was able to recover his original investment and to draw a salary for himself and his family which was rather more than he had previously earned. In 1973 he re-invested his original stake, as well as some more money, and increased his labour force to twelve people. In the next year a number of new warehouses were established in the area and Mr. Shah decided that this provided an opportunity for even further expansion.

He drew up a proposal for a loan of $4,000 to build a new workshop and to purchase new machinery. He submitted it to a bank and they were convinced that it was a viable proposition; they calculated that the new equipment would enable the production of the business to be tripled so that there would be no difficulty in repaying the loan and the 15% annual interest charge.

The loan was duly approved and disbursed and employment now increased to 22 people. Early in 1976, however, a competitive factory was set up nearby and Mr. Shah's business was only able to operate at 60% of its installed capacity. At the same time it suffered a further blow; the Town Planning Authorities decided to restrict the growth of warehousing activities in the city and to reserve the land for residential purposes. Stocks of unsold containers started to accummulate and the Drum Manufacturing Company began to lose money at an alarming rate. Mr. Shah could see that disaster was staring him in the face, and he applied to the local branch of a recently established Government agency devoted to assisting small-scale industries.

Mr. Shah's inquiry was enthusiastically received by one of the advisers in this centre, a certain Mr. Patel. He presented himself as philosopher, guide and friend to small industries and carried out a detailed analysis of the situation of the Drum Manufacturing Company. He produced an elaborate report with a two-fold solution under the headings of 'Diversification' and 'Equity Participation'. The existing production line was to be widened by the inclusion of milk churns, since a Dairy Development Corporation had recently been set up in the city.

The financial situation was to be improved by broadening the ownership base. The business was to be reconstituted as a joint venture between Mr. Shah and the State Small Industries Corporation. The total subscribed capital was to be $9,000. Mr. Patel recommended that Mr. Shah should raise his 50% share of this by selling work-in-progress and finished stocks from the Company, and the State Small Industries Corporation would be willing to make up any short-fall in his contribution if he could not raise the $4,500 he needed.

The Drum Manufacturing Company was duly reconstituted and Mr. Shah continued to run it in its new form. There was still a need for more capital; Mr. Patel approached a local bank and another State financial institution on Mr. Shah's behalf, and was able to persuade them to advance a loan of $30,000 to finance the diversification scheme, to renovate the existing machinery and to repair the building. They were willing to advance this money because the State Small Industries Corporation had demonstrated its faith in the enterprise by investing in its equity. Mr. Patel became the Chairman of the Board of Directors, Mr. Shah was the Managing Director and there were also representatives of the bank, the state small industries corporation and the other State financial institution.

In spite of all these arrangements, however, everything did not go according to plan. Mr. Shah was only able to raise $3,000 by selling some of the accumulated inventory, and the State Small Industries Corporation had to make up his contribution. The diversification was not a success, since the milk churns produced by the Company were of poor quality and over a third of them were rejected by their customers. Mr. Patel asked the Marketing Assistance Department of the State Small Industries Corporation to help the Drum Manufacturing Company. They approached public sector dairy corporations and co-operatives in other States and obtained a number of orders from them. Since these customers were unlikely to pay their bills promptly, and substantial investment was in any case required in raw material, the State Small Industries Corporation advanced a further $2,000 to the Drum Manufacturing Company to finance these orders. In spite of all this help, the Company failed to produce sufficient churns to satisfy the orders, and over a third of those they did produce were still rejected. Mr. Patel brought in experts from the Production Assistance Department of the State Small Industries Corporation. They examined the situation and made specific recommendations for improving quality. These could not, however, be implemented without more skilled workers and quality control staff, and these people required higher wages than had previously been paid. As a result losses increased still further and although quality was marginally improved the accumulated deficit now amounted to nearly $50,000.

Both the bank and the other state financial institution were becoming concerned about the arrears on their loans, and they approached the State Small Industries Corporation to see what could be done. The senior officials of the Corporation decided that an alternative view might be needed; they retained a firm of private consultants who investigated the complete business, from the point of view of personnel, management, production and marketing, and concluded that the basic problem was mismanagement. The State Small Industries Corporation was by this time heavily committed in terms of equity investment, its own loans and its unwritten guarantees to the other public sector investors. They felt that they had four alternatives; they could take the Company and run it themselves, they could in some way improve Mr. Shah's ability to manage it effectively, they could wind up the Company and sell the assets, or they could continue as they were, trying to improve the situation.

Comment

As in previous cases, the Drum Manufacturing Company was soundly established in the beginning and prospered in its early stages. Mr. Shah was apparently able to manage an enterprise employing five people without too much difficulty, and even when it expanded to twelve he had no problem.

The major expansion which he undertook with the help of bank finance proved to be too optimistic. As so often happens, the pioneer enterprise in a particular field chose to expand at exactly the same time as new competitors entered the field, so that Mr. Shah was faced with an expansion of his capacity at the same time as a contraction in demand. It may well be, however, that an enterprise employing 22 people was in fact beyond his managerial capacity, and this may have been a more fundamental problem than the decline in demand.

The assistance from the State Small Industries Corporation, although offered with the best of intentions, was in the event worse than useless. The initial analysis seems to have been carried out in a piecemeal way, without appreciating the fact that a small enterprise of this sort is an integrated whole, and cannot be treated in any other way. Management is the unifying factor which makes a success out of the enterprise; attempts to deal with marketing problems, policy, shortage of finance and production as if they were separate water-tight compartments only exaggerates the difficulties of the Manager who must run the enterprise as a whole.

It appears that Mr. Patel virtually took over the overall direction of the enterprise, without having the stimulus of personal financial commitment, and Mr. Shah must have felt increasingly bewildered as more experts and more institutions were brought into the picture. When his problems began, he only owed the bank $4,000 and had a reasonably small amount of his own money at risk. After receiving all this assistance, over $40,000 of his own and other institutions' money was tied up, and the management problems were enormously more complex.

It is easy to attempt to explain how a certain situation has arisen, but more difficult to recommend what should be done to remedy it. The best way out of the problem might be for the State Small Industries Corporation to take over the obligations of the other institutions in order to simplify the financial structure. They should then allow Mr. Shah the chance to manage the business without interference so that he can demonstrate his ability to put the situation right. If he fails, the Corporation would probably be best advised to sell the assets of the business to somebody more capable of managing them.

THE DUKAWA LEATHER WORKERS SOCIETY, NIGERIA

Hand-made leather goods have for many years been a traditional product of the Kano area of Nigeria, and there are large numbers of individual craftsmen engaged in this work on their own. The Government of Nigeria has always supported co-operatives as a means of enabling farmers and others to improve their livelihood, and the Government of the State of Kano vigorously supports this policy. Many of the leather workers found it difficult to market their products, and the Co-operative Department, which is part of the State Ministry of Trade, Industry and Co-operatives, set up the Kano Co-operative Federation in order to help leather workers and other small-scale artisans who had similar problems. The Federation purchased leather products from individual craftsmen, and was able to market them successfully because of the scale of its operation. Problems arose, however, because the Federation had to deal with so many individual craftsmen. The General Manager of the Federation therefore asked the Ministry to promote a co-operative for the leather workers. They argued that it would be easier for the Federation to buy its products from one source, rather than from large numbers of individuals, and in addition he felt that such a society would be able to organize local marketing itself, since the Federation had numerous other calls on its resources.

It would also be possible for such a co-operative to make use of the variety of financial, training and other services which were available to co-operatives in the State, but could not be provided to individuals and were difficult to access through a large union such as the Federation.

A Co-operative Officer was assigned to the task; he met with a number of leather workers, and succeeded in persuading them to register the Dukawa Leather Workers Society in January 1980. The Society started very well; the members were able to sell more of their products through the Federation and they also opened a small retail shop in the Dukawa area of Kano City to cater to the wealthy business people who visited Kano from neighbouring States. They also rented a shop at a hotel in the city, to cater for the tourist market, and as a result of their success their membership rose to over 200 craftsmen.

The Society continued to prosper for some two years, and in 1982 the Co-operative Department was further encouraged in its efforts to develop this Society when the Federal Government decided that leather work should be especially promoted as part of national policy to recognise particular crafts as a way of preserving national identity and resisting the pace of westernization. Towards the end of 1982, however, the Society started to decline. They ceased supplying leather work to the Co-operative Federation, they closed the shop at the hotel and there were no goods to be seen on display at the Dukawa shop. Members had clearly lost their enthusiasm.

The Co-operative Officer was in close contact with the Society and he had meetings with some of the Committee Members to discuss the problem. It appeared that their difficulties arose from the lack of raw materials and insufficient capital. They discussed the situation together, and decided to put forward a number of suggestions as a basis for reviving the Society.

Members had apparently not been attending meetings; the Officer recommended that the original Committee Members should re-organize the management of the Society, and should take it upon themselves to learn how to deal with problems of this sort in the future. He offered to organize seminars, to be conducted by the Education Section of the Ministry, in order to help the members to learn how to manage their enterprise.

The Society had been buying leather for its members from traditional local tanneries whose capacity was limited because they relied on skilled manual labour rather than machinery. The Co-operative Officer therefore offered to introduce the Society to some of the modern tanneries in the State, in order to guarantee reliable supplies of leather in the future. He also suggested that they should re-stock the shop in Dukawa and re-open the outlet at the hotel. He said he would contact another hotel in the city, and the Kano Tourist Centre, in order to ask them to open shops for the Society, and he would ask the Municipal Council to supply a plot of land in the famous Kurmi Market, so that the Society could open yet another shop there.

It was clear that all this could not be carried out with the funds presently at the disposal of the Society, which were insufficient even for its current level of operation. The Society's liabilities were legally limited to $100 per member, and in any case none of the members had actually paid for his share at all. The Officer therefore suggested that the members should be asked to pay what they owed for their shares and, if necessary, be requested to contribute further funds for the Society's operation. If they were unable to contribute enough money, he would help them apply for a loan from the Co-operative Bank, through the Co-operative Union, and, if possible, for a grant from the Government.

The Co-operative Officer now had to prepare a feasibility study, showing the extent to which the Society was able to finance its own resources, and demonstrating that it would be able to repay any loans which were necessary. Loans made through co-operative unions by the Co-operative Bank are generally guaranteed by the State Government and the Co-operative Officer has therefore to supervise societies in their use of monies which are leant to them. Because of the national significance of leathercraft, and the importance of co-operatives for national development, the Dukawa Leather Workers Society is regarded as a test case and its future will have great significance for the future of the co-operative movement as a whole in Nigeria.

Comment

Co-operatives that are started as a result of Government promotion, as opposed to independent initiative by the members, generally fail. It is therefore refreshing to find this example of a society which owes its origins entirely to official suggestions, but nevertheless succeeded, at least for its first two years. We are given no information about how the official recognition of the national importance of leatherwork was translated into actual assistance for the Co-operative in 1982, but it is tempting to wonder whether an excess of official intervention might have had something to do with the decline of the Society, particularly after its members had succeeded so well for the first two years.

Members' apathy may arise from a number of different causes, but if their Society is genuinely helping them to earn a better living, they are unlikely to lose interest in it. As with any business, it is important to ask whether the need for which the Society was originally started exists any more. It may be that members have succeeded in finding satisfactory alternative sources of supply, and outlets, or that they have been employed by private businesses at wages which offer an improvement on what they were able to earn on their own. If there really is no further need for the Co-operative's services, neither Government nor anyone else should invest time or money in trying to prolong its existence.

The information suggests, however, that the major problem is raw material; independent craftsmen, and co-operative societies which they themselves manage, sometimes find it difficult to form business relationships with large-scale modern units, which are used to operating with formal procedures that are often daunting to traditional craftsmen and others with little formal education. The Co-operative Officer can play a very useful role in overcoming these barriers, by introducing the Society to modern tanneries and helping both sides to overcome any reluctance they may have in dealing with the other. It may also be appropriate for the Co-operative Officer to assist in overcoming the same type of barrier between the Society and the Municipal Authorities, but it is important that the Co-operative should not receive any preference over other types of enterprise. The Co-operative Department's role is to ensure that co-operatives are not in any way disadvantaged, but there is no reason why they should receive particular privileges.

The specific suggestions put forward by the Co-operative Officer appear somewhat ambitious; problems in any enterprise can usually be traced to inadequate management. The proposed increase in the number of marketing outlets, and additional finance, will increase the size of the enterprise that has to be managed, and thus the complexity of its management; it may be advisable to move more slowly and to start by helping the Society to improve its supplies of raw material. This may in turn require additional finance, but this should if at all possible be obtained from members, using the savings they should have accumulated over the last two years, since the administrative problems involved in bank finance are likely to prove a substantial burden on management. Once the problem of raw material supply has been solved, it may then be appropriate to expand the marketing operation. The Co-operative Officer responsible for assisting this Society, and his superiors at the Department, must avoid the temptation to take over the management of the Society completely in their enthusiasm to create a 'model' as an example of co-operative success to the rest of the country. If the Society succeeded on this basis, it would be impossible to devote the same level of assistance to any larger number of co-operatives, and success would in fact be very unlikely since people who are outside a society, and employed by Government, are generally unable to maintain member enthusiasm and run an effective society.

THE ETHIOPIAN HANDICRAFTS CENTRE, ETHIOPIA

The Ethiopian Handicrafts Centre was originally established some 40 years ago and was then known as the Empress Menen Handicraft School. Its objective was to train young Ethiopians in a variety of handicraft skills, and there were initially eleven different workshops in the School. The most important ones were blacksmithing, carpet making, jewellery, pottery, carpentry and knitting. The School never kept an accurate record of how many people were trained, but there is no doubt that many hundreds of people went through its courses over the years.

Around 1965 the School opened a small retail shop within its premises in order to market some of the items which the students were making during their training. This seemed to be a good idea, both in order to raise some revenue and to ensure that the students appreciated the requirements of the market-place, but a number of serious problems arose as a result.

Because the senior students and staff were producing a number of very high quality handicraft items, the shop attracted large numbers of customers, including the aristocracy and members of the family of Haile Selasie, who was at that time Emperor of Ethiopia. The management of the School realized that sales of this sort could generate substantial revenue, both for the operation of the School and for their own benefit. They decided slightly to alter the curriculum so that the students were made to spend more time on the production of saleable items instead of devoting their time to developing their skills through training. Demand continued to grow, especially for carpets, and the School's very highest quality carpets became the favourite gift which the Emperor used to present to Heads of Government and other dignitaries he visited in Africa and beyond.

In order to meet the increasing demand for high quality carpets and jewellery from the Imperial Court and the aristocracy, the School gradually scaled down and finally totally abandoned training, turning all its facilities over to production. Most of the other Departments were closed and their instructors were transferred to the Carpet Department. More workers were employed and the School turned over to two shift operations.

By 1974 there was a total of 450 workers in what was still called the Handicrafts School. Most of them were employed on a temporary basis and were paid very low piece-work wages based on the amount and quality of the work they produced. The workers had no long term security of employment, and although many of them had worked in the School for over ten years they were still regarded as temporary workers. They were naturally aggrieved that under the Imperial Regime there was little they could do.

The Revolution started in 1974 and the Emperor dissolved the old Government and appointed a new and more liberal one. The workers in the School petitioned the Government to be made permanent employees able to earn fixed salaries. The Government was anxious to ingratiate itself with the people and therefore granted the workers' demands; they effectively became permanently employed civil servants.

Almost at once the workers' productivity dropped drastically. There was an enormous increase in absenteeism and because of the drop in production, and the general disruption caused by the Revolution, the School incurred losses of approximately $100,000 in 1975. In 1977 the Government set up the Handicrafts and Small Industries Development Agency to promote local crafts and small industries. Because there was no other obvious home for the Handicrafts School, the Government decided that it should be taken over by the new Agency.

The Agency was only a promotional and assistance organization, with no authority itself to produce or market handicrafts or anything else. If it was to retain control of the School, it was therefore necessary fundamentally to change the nature of its operation. As a first step the School was renamed the Ethiopian Handicrafts Centre, and it was planned to turn it into a Centre for the development and testing of improved technologies, for providing skills training to rural artisans and entrepreneurs and as an emporium for the demonstration of products and tools.

This appeared to be the best policy, and would in addition provide a facility which was badly needed. Unfortunately, however, if it was to be carried through about 300 of the 350 remaining workers would have to be dismissed. This could not be done since they were civil servants and other jobs would have to be found for them in the public service. For two years the Agency attempted to place the workers through the Personnel Administration Office of the Government, but because their skills were basically unsuitable for Government jobs they were only able to find jobs for six of them. Meanwhile, carpets continued to be produced. Because of low productivity, uncertainty about the future and the disappearance of the main source of demand for the highest price carpets, the Centre continued to lose money at a rate of between $60,000 and $100,000 per year.

Comment

If handicraft training is carried out in isolation from the market-place, it is likely to become sterile and irrelevant. It is therefore wise to ensure that trainees are in touch with the market-place, and there are few better ways of doing this than by allowing training institutions to operate their own retail outlets. Students can then themselves observe customers' reactions, and can obtain experience in the business aspects of their craft.

In this particular case, perhaps because of inadequate funding for the School and poor supervision of its managers, the situation was allowed to get out of control. The School was run mainly for the benefit of its managers, who appear to have exploited the traditional skills of their workforce.

The School was nevertheless a large employer of labour, and there is no evidence that its workers were compelled to remain there. There were presumably no preferable alternative employment opportunities for them, so they were willing to stay in spite of the apparent exploitation. The managers behaved no differently from what might be expected of private entrepreneurs, and the only major difference was that they were actually misusing the Government's property.

After the Revolution, the School lost its major market and it obviously became necessary for it to change its products and also to alter its employment policies because of the new-found strength of trade unions. Little attention appears to have been paid, however, to marketing policy, and the workers' conditions moved from one extreme to another. Although it may be uncomfortable for those who are personally involved, insecurity is in a sense one of the major benefits of small enterprises. They must be flexible and respond rapidly to change and competition, or their owners and their employees will lose their jobs. The staff of many Government organizations, including those responsible for promoting small enterprises, might well perform more effectively if they too stood to lose their jobs if they did not provide an effective service. Life-long security of employment is not always in the national interest in public administration, but it is never appropriate in a manufacturing enterprise.

Many of the case studies in this book describe the problems which have arisen when official promotion organizations become involved in the actual ownership and management of business enterprises. The Government of Ethiopia was correct in excluding direct operations of this sort from the brief of the Handicrafts and Small Industries Development Agency, but it is unfortunate that the School has been allocated to an Agency which has no way of continuing to offer employment to its craftsmen. It would probably be better to reconstitute the School as an independent manufacturing enterprise, owned by its workers as a co-operative, by private investors or, in the last resort, by Government. It may be difficult to deprive the workers of their job security, but it is grossly unfair that any group should enjoy this privilege, particularly in a small country. The School should be formally recognized as a manufacturing enterprise, and should be allowed to operate as independently as possible, under whatever form of ownership is appropriate.

THE GAMBIAN ARTISANS' MARKETING CO-OPERATIVE, THE GAMBIA

The Gambia is a small country on the west coast of Africa whose people have until recently been almost wholly dependent on groundnuts. The country has very little rain, which is not reliable, and the production of the staple crop can therefore be halved in drought years. The country is amongst the least developed nations in the world, and the Government is therefore anxious to develop new ways by which people could improve their standard of living.

The country has wide unspoiled sandy beaches on the Atlantic coast, and these started in the 1970s to be developed for international tourism. Because of the short flight from Europe, low labour costs and efficient operations the country rapidly developed into a major tourist destination.

The people of this part of West Africa have a long tradition of indigenous handicrafts in a variety of fields. These include tie-dyed batik and hand-woven fabrics, traditional clothing and leather articles, silver jewellery, musical instruments, carvings, baskets and pottery. The Government realized that these traditional handicrafts could provide a means whereby a far larger number of people would be able to benefit from the tourist trade, in addition to those who were actually employed in the hotels and so on. The Indigenous Business Advisory Service, which is a Government organization devoted to assisting local small enterprise, promoted the establishment of the Gambian Artisans' Marketing Co-operative (GAMCO) in 1977. Its main purpose was to provide a market for the large numbers of independent craftsmen, and in order to do this the Society opened a modern retail outlet in the main tourist area of the country. They also provided assistance in product design, quality control and advertizing for the craftsmen, and they ran training courses in production techniques and management skills.

These activities were generally successful, and the Society introduced a savings and loan scheme and a raw materials supply service for their members, and they started to develop export outlets in order to avoid the seasonal pattern which was imposed on them by their reliance on tourists who visited The Gambia.

Before the establishment of GAMCO handicrafts were sold only through local markets and by street traders. Since the GAMCO shop has been opened, tourists and foreign residents of the country have been able to buy quality products at set prices and sales have also continued during the off season, when there are very few tourists but when local residents are still interested in buying handicrafts. As a result GAMCO has been able to buy several thousand dollars' worth of handicrafts from its members during this time of year when they would usually have no income at all apart from their small farms.

By 1982 there were approximately 400 members; those who lived near the GAMCO shop delivered their products themselves and were paid in cash or by credit according to the liquidity position of the Society at that time. GAMCO collected handicrafts from the majority of members who lived in more remote areas, and the collection staff took the opportunity of informing members about current market trends at the same time as they collected their goods.

At the beginning GAMCO was managed by an expatriate volunteer from the United States, who had many years of experience managing his own business and a number of co-operatives. Between 1977 and 1979 he was assisted by another volunteer who was responsible for training the members, and a British volunteer was also recruited to act as store buyer and quality controller. The Society also employed a local part-time clerk and a part-time tailor to make up some of the fabrics into ready-to-wear garments.

In 1978 a Gambian manager was appointed. He had a Certificate in Co-operative Studies and had worked in the Department of Co-operatives for some 15 years. He worked together with the foreign volunteer for somewhat over a year, and a local accountant was appointed at that time. The volunteers then had to leave, and the local managers took over full responsibility for the Society. The Indigenous Business Advisory Service continued to advise the managers, and to provide extension and training to GAMCO members in rural areas.

At the end of the 1981–2 financial year, GAMCO employed the Manager and the Accountant, five sales girls, the tailor, the driver and two support staff. The Indigenous Business Advisory Service paid the salaries of the Manager, the Accountant and the driver and the wages for the rest of the staff had to be met out of GAMCO's surplus.

The Society had originally been started with the help of a grant of $5,000 from a United States assistance agency. This was used to lease and renovate the shop, and to provide initial working capital. Shortly thereafter a loan of $9,000 was obtained from the local Development Bank, in order to finance working capital, and this loan had almost entirely been repaid by the end of 1979. The Society achieved a net surplus of almost $10,000 in the year ending March 1980, and its successful results were considered most creditable for a newly established business, particularly since its objec-

GAMCO Profit and Loss Account for the Years Ending June, 1982, 1981 and 1980

	1981/82		1980/81		1979/80	
	$	$	$	$	$	$
Sales		36,000		61,000		71,000
Cost of Goods Sold		27,000		47,000		50,000
Gross Surplus		9,000		14,000		21,000
Expenses						
Wages and Salaries	9,500		7,500		4,800	
Rent	2,100		2,100		1,700	
Miscellaneous Expenses	2,300		2,400		3,300	
Bank Interest	1,500		600		100	
Looting	8,000		nil		nil	
Total Expenses		23,400		12,600		9,900
Surplus/Loss		$ (14,400)		$ 1,400		$ 11,100

GAMCO Balance Sheets as at 30 June, 1982, 1981 and 1980

Liabilities	1982	1981	1980
	$	$	$
Members' Investment	900	900	900
Accumulated Surplus	5,500	19,900	18,500
Bank Overdraft	21,500	7,000	8,000
Accounts Payable	1,000	600	700
Total Liabilities	$28,900	$28,400	$28,100

Assets			
	$	$	$
Office Equipment (after depreciation)	1,600	2,000	2,200
Prepaid Expenses	600	500	1,300
Loans to Members	14,200	8,800	9,400
Stocks of Goods for Resale	8,200	12,700	6,300
Trade Debtors	4,100	3,300	3,900
Cash	200	1,100	5,000
Total Assets	$28,900	$28,400	$28,100

tives were not only to make a surplus but also to provide a social service to its members.

Because of the Society's success the management were able to negotiate an overdraft facility of up to $25,000 from the local bank, after clearing off the initial loan; this was guaranteed under a United Nations scheme which was operated by the Indigenous Business Advisory Service.

After the middle of 1980 the results started to deteriorate; less attention was paid to quality control and the management of stocks, and administrative expenses also rose very sharply without any corresponding increase in business. There was also some internal disorder in The Gambia during 1981 and approximately $8,000 worth of goods were looted from the Society's store at this time. As a result of this and other problems, it can be seen from the accounts which follow that the Society incurred a loss of some $15,000 during the year ended March 1982.

In spite of its initial success it appears that there were a number of long-standing problems which revealed themselves after the first year or two and which must be solved before the Society can be considered totally viable. Some 80% of the members are illiterate and most of them still fail to understand the principle of the Co-operative. Some refuse to sell their best goods to the Society, because they believe that it exists only to make a profit for its own staff, while others argue that the Society should accept everything they make, regardless of its quality, because they are, they argue, its members.

The savings and loan scheme has proved very difficult to operate, because so many of the members are ignorant of banking procedures, and very few of the members ever bother to come to meetings. Since some of them believe that that the purpose of the Society is to exploit them, while others think that the Society has an obligation to buy everything they make, they feel that there is no reason why they should have anything to do with its management.

Comment

This Co-operative Society was started entirely as a result of Government initiative, and the leadership never came from within the membership. At first, the managers did not even come from the same country; when they left, they were replaced by professional managers who had little in common with the artisan members.

There is no doubt, however, that the craftsmen themselves would never have started a co-operative, or otherwise improved the marketing of their handicrafts, and it is clear that they benefitted

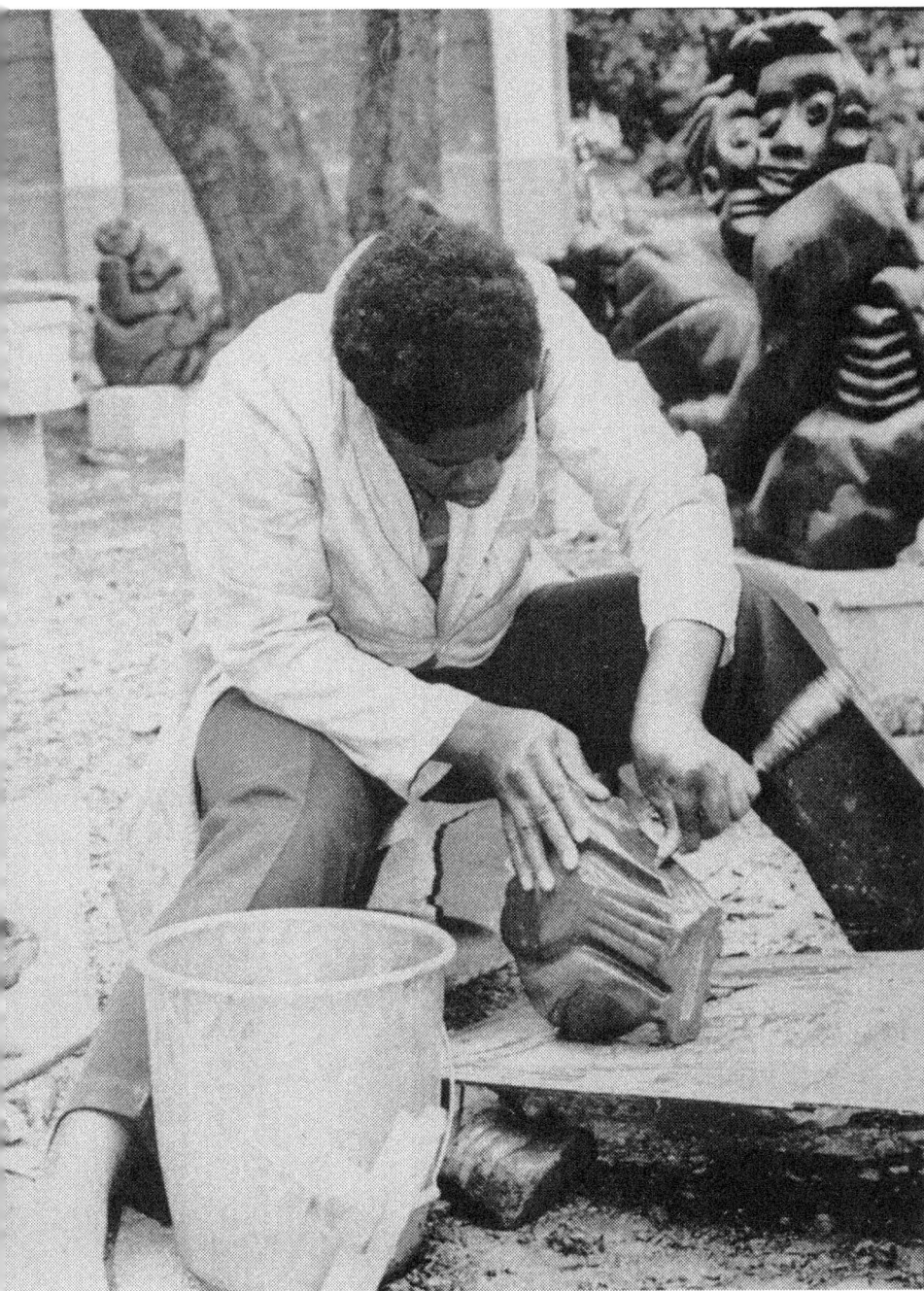

*A sculptor in Harare (a member of the Canon Patterson
Co-operative, case study number four).*

Partners in carpentry.

*The co-operative steel mill in Sri Lanka
(photo. S.M.J. Neangoda).*

substantially from the early success of the Society. It was not really a Co-operative Society in the genuine sense of the word at all, so much as a Government supported purchasing and marketing department. It served the members, like any other Government Department, but was in no sense directed or controlled by them.

It may be perfectly reasonable for Government to spend money on an activity of this sort, although civil servants are not generally very successful marketers. It could be argued that it is wrong to call such an organization a co-operative society at all, until or unless it develops into an organization which is genuinely run by its members, since people will come to think that co-operatives normally function like GAMCO, and will never realize the potential of co-operatives as a real form of self-help.

The loss incurred by GAMCO as a result of looting should probably be refunded by Government, if it is not already covered by insurance. Otherwise, however, the objective should be gradually to reduce the level of subsidy so that the Society can develop its ability to stand on its own feet, at the same time as its members become capable of managing it.

It is always difficult to judge the point at which a co-operative society, or any other form of Government inspired business enterprise, should be set loose from Government support and allowed to sink or swim. Five years may not be enough, particularly in view of the set-back caused by civil disorder in 1981, but it is in any case unwise to build a very complex organization, with a number of different functions, if it is eventually to be handed over to people who have only a very rudimentary idea of management. The Society now consists of a small raw material supply business, a purchasing and collection system, a retail shop and a savings and loan operation. It may be appropriate to 'privatize' one or more of these quite separate operations, in order to simplify the management task. The retail shop is clearly an enterprise which would be more likely to be run economically under private ownership, and it may also be possible to hand over the savings and loan operation to a commercial bank. The raw material supply service is more or less dormant in any case, and the Society would thus be left with the purchasing and collection task which is particularly valuable and would form a very suitable basis for a real co-operative enterprise. It could then later diversify into other related activities, once members had developed the capacity to direct it properly.

THE JAFAU CO-OPERATIVE HANDICRAFT SOCIETY, FIJI

Fiji consists of some 500 islands in the south-west Pacific. Approximately 100 of these are inhabited, and the total population is well under one million. Many of the people in the outer islands are still subsistence farmers, but in addition to sugar and coconut plantations, there is a growing tourist industry; this has led to an increasing demand for local handicrafts.

The island of Jafau is approximately 150 kilometres from Viti Levu, the largest island in the group where the capital city of Suva is situated. The people of Jafau have traditionally been expert wood carvers. For many years they used to send their carvings to Suva and the other tourist centres in Viti Levu by sea. As land became scarce in their own island, because of the growth of population, the wood carvers came to rely more and more on the money they could earn from selling their carvings and a group of them decided to move to Viti Levu in order to be able to set up a full-time wood carving industry together.

They settled on the southern coast of Viti Levu, close to the tourist hotels. They carried on operating in the same way for many years and because the tourists were very happy to buy their carvings their business grew every year. The tourists were interested to see the carvings actually being produced, and also expressed an interest in other traditional activities of the people. The carvers invited a number of women who were experts in the traditional dances of their home island of Jafau to join them, and they together used to offer regular dancing entertainment to the tourists at their hotels. The tourists paid well for the entertainment, and in addition they bought more carvings as a result of seeing more of the traditional activities of the people who produced them.

The group continued to expand and by 1980 they were offering dancing exhibitions and displays of carvings in a number of the leading hotels. They then felt that they should have a place of their own where tourists could observe the carvers at work and buy carvings and other handicrafts. They also felt that there would be a market for a coffee bar and a general retail store, and they wished to make a small museum out of the collection of old carvings and other handicrafts which they had accumulated over the years. They felt that a collection of this sort would be a valuable contribution to the cultural heritage of the island, as well as being a tourist attraction.

One of the members of the group had had some training in an architect's drawing office. He drew some outline plans of a building to accommodate all the various activities they had in mind, and made some estimates of the amount of materials needed and of the cost of constructing the building. The members agreed that they themselves would contribute their labour free of charge but the cost of all the materials, and of a suitable plot, was far beyond their own resources. They had no formal organization of any sort, and they wondered how they should go about acquiring the necessary funds to construct the building that they felt they needed.

Comment

This group of carvers had its origins in an informal association of people who came together because they shared similar skills. Because they had already formed a viable association on the basis of their part-time activity, they were able to escape from the growing hardship of subsistence farming and to move as a group to a location nearer to their market. Unlike many individuals who move from rural areas to the city, these people were able to maintain and indeed improve their livelihood because it was already soundly established.

The group was not originally promoted by any co-operative department or ministry, nor was it established in order to take advantage of any preferential loan terms or other assistance. A number of people, with similar skills, came together because they realized that they could do better as a group than as individuals.

The group seems to have succeeded very well in Viti Levu, partly perhaps because they were strangers from another island. They seem to have been able to exploit the tourist demand for their carvings, and for traditional entertainment, without losing their respect for the traditions of their people. Unlike many similar groups, prosperity has not led to disunity, and they have even been able to take in women who had different skills and to include them in their activities.

Now, however, they have reached a stage where formalization is needed if they are to obtain access to institutional funds and construct the building they want. They have so far survived and prospered without the benefits of formal incorporation, but if they are to expand as they wish they must take the risk of moving from an informal association to a formal co-operative society. Any outside advice and assistance should be strictly limited; the association should, only if they wish, be advised on the feasibility or otherwise of their proposed building, and on the procedures whereby they can formalize their association and thus become eligible for a loan. They, and their advisers, must be aware of the dangers of buildings of this sort; co-operatives and similar organizations often construct what are really no more than monuments to their own success, although they may delude themselves that they are important facilities for their continued prosperity. They must ensure that the tourists will really wish to visit the proposed building, and that they will be able to organize and manage its regular maintenance and operation, before going through the procedures which must precede raising finance for its construction.

THE JUMBIE HOUSE POTTERY, DOMINICA

Dominica is a small island in the southern Caribbean, with a total population of under 100,000 people. There are few local industries, since most of the people depend on subsistence agriculture, together with some tourism and a few cash crops such as limes and bananas.

There is a severe unemployment problem, paticularly amongst young people, and in 1974 an expert from the International Labour Office of the United Nations started a group training project in ceramics at Jumbie House on the northwest coast of the island. The location was chosen because of the excellent clay which was available there and because there were large numbers of unemployed young people living in the neighbourhood who were interested in learning how to make pottery. The objective was eventually to develop a viable ceramic industry on the island to provide job opportunities, to use local raw materials and to provide locally manufactured pottery to replace imports.

The project started in 1974 with a group of 30 young men and women. By the middle of the following year ten of them had left, and the numbers fell later to 15 because they could not earn a steady income. A number of those who left had joined the project under the impression that they would be paid a regular salary and left when they discovered that it was intended to be a self-supporting industry.

The International Labour Office expert found it a continuous struggle to maintain the enthusiasm of the group, because he only had a small amount of money with which to pay them and although some pottery was sold they could not really achieve a viable volume, or manufacture goods of high quality, because they did not have a suitable kiln.

At the end of 1975 the expert had to leave Dominica, and the whole project was assigned to the Youth Division of the Government of Dominica. At this time there were four girls and eight young men still working there, and one of them had emerged as the most skilled and most able to manage the activities of the rest. Although they lacked all the equipment they needed, they were able to make a fairly wide range of products and these were gradually becoming known on the island. Although they never worked at full capacity for more than a few weeks at a time, they demonstrated that they were able to produce at a rate which would have achieved sales of around $18,000 a year, for a total of 4,000 pieces. These included teapots, teacups and saucers, a range of flower-pots and vases, ashtrays, lamps, ornaments and various other containers.

The major problem was firing the products and just before the expert left he had helped the group to place an order for an electric kiln which would be big enough to fire and glaze everything they produced. They had hoped that a donor could be found to pay for the kiln but this unfortunately proved impossible. When the Youth Division took over they were determined to make the group self-sufficient as quickly as possible and attempted to raise money with this end in view. They sent two members of the group to be trained in Jamaica under a scheme sponsored by the Commonwealth Fund for Technical Co-operation.

The Youth Division commissioned a study by a local firm of management consultants in order to establish the need for a kiln. They submitted the application for funding to Christian Action for Development in the Eastern Caribbean (CADEC) who agreed to support the group but said that they could only afford a wood-fired kiln rather than an electric one.

The group tried to explain to the funding agency that there was not a readily available supply of firewood, and the Chief Forest Officer of the island supported their view. The expert who advised CADEC did not agree, however, and the Jumbie House Pottery group eventually agreed to accept a wood-fired kiln. In the meantime, they carried on with their plans to obtain finance and other facilities for the workshop in order to establish it properly.

Many months went by and the kiln had not arrived. The members of the group found it difficult to contact the funding agency, which was based in Jamaica, since they were remote even from the capital city of Dominica. They were very anxious to establish their venture as a self-supporting viable enterprise, in order to employ as many young people as possible and to save foreign exchange, but they felt that no one was able to help them to overcome their problems. They contacted the funding agency and other organizations but without success and a number of them wondered whether they should leave and try to find something else to do.

Comment

In circumstances of this sort, where there is little or no local industry and unemployment among young people is a major problem, it is clearly necessary for Government agencies to take the initiative. It may not have been clear from the beginning that the Jumbie House

Pottery was intended to be a business rather than merely a training school, but this lack of clarity may also be excused since it may be that it would have been impossible to recruit people if it had been clear from the outset that they had to earn their own living.

The loss of members of the group may actually have been a good thing, since those that remained were probably those who were most committed and enthusiastic. It appears that one person emerged as some sort of informal leader but the continuing involvement first of the expert from the International Labour Office and then of the Youth Division may have deprived the group of the feeling that they were themselves responsible for their own destiny, and of the impetus to allow one of their members actually to be a genuine leader.

As in other cases, it may well be that support was continued too long; if the group had been left on their own after the departure of the expert from the International Labour Office, it might well have been that the informal leader would have taken over and would even have had the initiative to construct a wood-fired kiln out of local materials since very little outside assistance is required to construct a wood-fired kiln beyond the correct design. An electric kiln might have been more desirable, but if no external assistance was available the group might have realized that they could not hope for this at once and should in the short term at least be contented with one which was fired with wood.

If craft training is provided in a purely academic way, and no attempt is made to produce items for sale, trainees are unlikely to attain the necessary standards or to realize how they will have to operate in the real world. On the other hand, it is difficult to make a training venture self-supporting from the outset and it may be that in this case, through the premature withdrawal of the International Labour Office expert, that the group was forced to become self-supporting too soon. A point must always come, however, when external support has to be withdrawn and a venture such as this must 'sink or swim'. If it succeeds, all is well and if it fails it may well be that the trainees will find employment elsewhere, some perhaps on their own, while the venture itself as originally envisaged might not have been viable in any case.

THE LANKA STEEL CO-OPERATIVE, SRI LANKA

Early in 1970 a small steel mill which had for many years operated in a southern suburb of Colombo, in Sri Lanka, ran into difficulties. The mill employed some 50 people, and used to manufacture steel reinforcing bars for building construction, using wheels, rails and other scrap materials from the Sri Lankan railway.

Because of poor management, production had fallen to around 50 tons a month, only slightly more than half what was possible, and a severe shortage of raw materials developed. The management had in any case lost interest in the enterprise, the equipment was old and in need of repair, and they decided to close the business down.

This was a severe blow to the employees and the local community. Two of the redundant workers, one of whom had been the Superintendent of the small labour force and the other the Assistant Production manager, were particularly resourceful and determined. They realized that the work force had included a number of skilled and very conscientious people, and they concluded that it would be possible to bring the unit back into production if only they could obtain enough finance and recruit a competent manager. They spoke to a number of the other people who had lost their jobs, and they all expressed their willingness to commit whatever savings they had to the revival of the enterprise. Nevertheless, the group could not possibly muster enough funds from its own resources to reopen the mill, and the problems appeared insurmountable.

The two leaders were determined to persevere. They realized that political patronage was essential for the success of any venture of this sort in Sri Lanka, and they decided to approach the Member of Parliament for the constituency in which the mill was located. He was happy to help, since the mill was an important source of jobs in his constituency and a number of the redundant workers had already made the situation known to him. He knew that he could benefit the people, and his own reputation, if he was associated with a co-operative venture of this sort.

The two initiators of the venture realized that one of the reasons for the past problems at the mill had been the lack of commitment and interest on the part of the workers. They had come to appreciate that most of the work force were people of some competence and initiative, who were not only very good at their jobs but could also make some contribution to the management of the enterprise if they were given a chance. They therefore decided that every worker would have a personal stake in the enterprise and a say in its direction, and they agreed with the workers that each would contribute $100 towards the initial share capital, giving a total of $5,000.

They also realized that $5,000 was not enough money with which to restart operations. They still had a need for management expertise and for practical expressions of commitment from the suppliers of raw material and other institutions which could influence the success of the operation. They therefore invited a number of influential people to join the Board. These included representatives of the Co-operative Marketing Federation and the Co-operative Industries Union, two people who were nominated by the Member of Parliament and a senior staff member of the Sri Lanka Steel Corporation, who were the suppliers of raw material. The two leaders made up the remaining members of the Board, and the outside institutions also contributed a total of $20,000 to the share capital. This made a total of $25,000, including the worker members' contribution, which was enough to start operations. Accordingly, the Lanka Steel Co-operative was incorporated in December 1972 and started operations early in the following year.

The outside representatives on the Board ensured that the Society enjoyed the good-will and services of their respective institutions, and they also gave management advice and assistance as required. The work force were totally committed and dedicated to the success of their business, and the new Co-operative was able to earn a profit in a very few months after starting operation. By 1978 they had accumulated earnings of $17,000 and were able to buy the equipment and the freehold of the premises, which they had up till then rented from the previous owners. By 1982 production had reached 80 tons a month and they were employing a total of 125 people, working in three shifts around the clock.

The original leaders appreciated that they lacked the necessary management expertise, and they recruited a professional manager and an accountant, to be responsible for the day-to-day running of the mill. Virtually all the original members remained with the business, and there was great competition for any vacancies that occurred. The wages were approximately the same as those paid in similar enterprises in the area, but worker members also received an incentive bonus of between $30 and $80 a month each, depending on the volume produced. They earned an additional $20 for good attendance, and food and medical allowances, and if results were satisfactory, as they generally were, they received two months additional wages in April and in December, as well as 35 days leave per year. Most employees in other co-operatives are only entitled to 27 days leave a year.

In its early years the Society enjoyed a protected market, since imports were heavily taxed. The Government later adopted a more open economic policy which meant that the Co-operative had to face competition from imported steel. In 1982 reinforcement bars from Japan were being landed at Colombo for $1,150 per ton whereas the Lanka Steel Co-operative's selling price was $1,200. The Board of Directors, however, was well aware of the problem. They were determined to overcome it and were investigating the possibilities of diversifying into building vehicle bodies and manufacturing steel gates and girders for construction purposes. They calculated that they would need about $100,000 for the necessary new equipment and the Board were confident that they could obtain the necessary amounts from their own resources and from outside institutions, because of their record of progress and sound financial management.

Comment

The purpose of most co-operative societies is to provide a service to their members which they are unable to provide for themselves. Farmers come together in order to purchase processing equipment or to market their crops, and handicraft producers form societies in order to buy raw material or to open a retail shop. The Lanka Steel Society is fundamentally different. It is an industrial or workers' co-operative, whose members have come together in order to finance and manage the enterprise in which they work. Members of a service co-operative retain their own independent activities, and only purchase certain services from it. The members of the Lanka Steel Co-operative rely on it for their complete livelihood.

Like most successful co-operatives, of either kind, this Society was initiated by its own members and not as a result of suggestions from outsiders. They were faced by a crisis, in that they had lost their jobs, and two leaders emerged who were willing to give their time and energy to organizing a society to save their own and their friends' employment.

Many co-operative societies are exploited by politicians and others for their own purposes. The leaders of the Lanka Steel Society might themselves be accused of exploiting powerful institutions and individuals, in that they appreciated the necessity for influence in high places and recruited powerful allies by offering them positions on the Board of Directors. The leaders and the members were also willing to recruit outsiders with the management skills they themselves did not possess. They paid them an economic salary, and were willing to take instructions from them

The Lanka Steel Co-operative Limited
Profit and Loss Account for the Year Ended 31 March 1982

	$	$
Sales		900,000
Expenses		
Raw materials	500,000	
Wages	110,000	
Salaries	6,000	
Administration	12,000	
Total Expenses		628,000
Surplus		272,000
Taxation		32,000
Net Surplus		$240,000

The Lanka Steel Co-operative Limited
Balance Sheet as at 31 March, 1982

Liabilities	$	Fixed Assets	$
Members' Capital		Land	16,000
Subscriptions	5,000	Steel Rolling Mills	54,000
Capital Subscribed		Other Plant and	
by Organizations	20,000	Equipment	25,000
Reinvested Earnings	234,000		
Accounts Payable	2,000	Current Assets	
		Finished Steel Stocks	50,000
		Raw Material Stocks	52,000
		Accounts Receivable	28,000
		Cash and Bank Balance	36,000
Total Liabilities	$261,000	Total Assets	$261,000

because they respected their expertise. Many co-operative societies fail because the members are unwilling to pay anybody more than they themselves receive, and thus deprive the society of the skills it needs.

The Society was able to benefit initially from the protected market, and did not have in its early stages to concern itself unduly with marketing problems. The shortage of raw materials had, however, partly contributed to the downfall of the previous owners, and the leaders dealt with this problem by involving their main supplier in the management and financing of the Society.

They appear, however, to be responding equally constructively to the threat of external competition. They now have the financial resources and standing necessary to finance their expansion into activities which are less subject to foreign competition, and it appears that the Society is likely to continue to prosper and to demonstrate that industrial co-operatives can succeed, given the right conditions and committed leadership.

NORTHERN TEXTILES,
BANGLADESH

Abdul Matin had for some years owned and operated a small trading business specializing mainly in cloth, and in 1964 he decided that he would like to start manufacturing. He was familiar with local tastes and wanted to produce sarees, plain cloth and striped and checked shirting since he knew that these would sell well. He approached the Bangladesh Small and Cottage Industries Corporation and with their help prepared a scheme for his proposed enterprise Northern Textiles. He started in a small way, and the total investment was only $12,300.

Matin had over the years saved a large proportion of the profits from his small trading business, and he was able to invest $4,100 in his enterprise; he borrowed a further $8,200 from the Small and Cottage Industries Corporation, so that he could invest the total of $12,300 in his new business. He spent $3,600 on land and buildings, $1,200 on office furniture and equipment and $6,300 on weaving equipment specially imported from Japan. This left $1,200 for working capital and he found that this was enough to start operations on a profitable basis. The loan from the Small and Cottage Industries Corporation was to be repaid over five years and they charged 7½% interest.

The business grew steadily over the next seven years. By the end of 1970 a total of 20 skilled and semi-skilled workers were employed, while Matin himself dealt with the management and marketing aspects of the enterprise because of his long experience in the textile trade. He had succeeded in repaying the loan on the terms agreed, and had negotiated further loans in order to purchase more equipment; at the end of 1970 he owed a total of $8,000 on these new loans.

In 1971, however, the Bangladesh Liberation War broke out and there was a total breakdown of law and order for some nine months during the year. Northern Textiles suffered very badly. The stock of finished goods, the raw materials, the spares and even some of the machinery were stolen by the occupation forces and other unscrupulous people, and during the whole period of the war the factory was closed. The business thus suffered heavy losses at this time.

At the end of the war the occupation armies left Bangladesh and Abdul Matin, like so many other business people in the country, found that his business was more or less destroyed. He had only his land and building and the few items of machinery that had not been stolen or damaged. His skill and persistence were unimpaired, however, and he was determined to start again. He successfully obtained an interest-free rehabilitation loan under a special scheme which the Government had started to assist businesses like Northern Textiles to start after the war. Matin re-engaged some of his workers and after making substantial efforts he managed to start the business once more early in 1972.

After the independence of Bangladesh, however, conditions became very difficult. Prices rose very steeply and it became almost impossible to obtain the imported spare parts which Matin needed to keep his equipment in working order. His employees needed to be paid more, because the cost of living had gone up so much, and there was a severe shortage of yarn which was the basic raw material of the business. Because of the damage which the machinery had suffered during the war, and the difficulty of obtaining spare parts, much of the machinery was not in working order. As a result the factory was out of balance and could not operate at full capacity, and in addition the electricity supply was most unreliable. Matin had insufficient working capital to pay his workers and to purchase raw material on the occasions when it was available, and the interest rate on his original loans from the Corporation was also increased at this time.

As a result of these problems Matin was unable to make repayments of the original loan as they fell due. When he was pressed for repayment by the Small and Cottage Industries Corporation he told them about all his problems and argued that it was surely unreasonable to expect him to be able to meet his obligations. The Staff of the Corporation, however, said that he had already received his interest free rehabilitation loan. They might be willing to discuss the possibility of providing further assistance, but only after he had successfully cleared off the loan he had obtained before the war.

They even threatened to auction off the equipment and the building if repayments on this loan were not received. Abdul Matin approached a number of other financial institutions but none of them was able to help him since he was already indebted to the Small and Cottage Industries Corporation. Abdul Matin needed extra finance merely to operate the business with its existing equipment. He was also faced with competition from new units which had been set up after the Liberation War and were equipped with more modern machinery. He had not calculated how much money would be needed totally to re-equip his factory, but he knew that it would be a very large sum and that it would eventually be necessary to make this investment if his business was to survive and prosper.

Matin felt that his case deserved special consideration; he had always lived very modestly, re-investing the vast majority of his profits in the business, and his workers agreed that he had been a model employer. He approached the Small and Cottage Industries Corporation once again, and asked them if they could possibly treat him as a special case. The staff of the Corporation responded quite favourably. They said that they would be very happy to help him to prepare a proposal both to acquire the finance necessary to establish his business on a sound footing, and to purchase new equipment in order to enable him to meet competition. They demanded, however, that he should first repay his old loan before they could consider any new financing. They were willing even to reschedule the interest which was due on the old loan, but the principal must first be repaid. In spite of all his determination, Abdul Matin was close to giving up. He could see no way in which he could raise $8,000, without selling what was left of his business, and this would defeat the whole object. There seemed to be no alternative, however, and he decided that this was the only way in which he could clear his debt, even though this would mean the destruction of his enterprise, the loss of everything he had worked for for so long, and unemployment for his workers.

Comment

Abdul Matin appears to have been a 'model entrepreneur' until the Bangladesh Liberation War. He started in trade, which requires very little capital or skill, and after acquiring knowledge of the textile business, and a certain amount of money, he moved into manufacturing. He surveyed the market carefully and produced products which were in demand, and employed large numbers of people with a very modest outlay of capital.

The Small and Cottage Industries Corporation played a vital role in his success, responding constructively to his original request for advice and funding, and providing further support as his business developed. It would be difficult to find a better example of the positive development role of the individual entrepreneur, or of effective co-operation between a small enterprise financing agency and an individual business person.

The Liberation War, however, with its attendant breakdown of law and order, changed the situation completely. The initial rehabilitation loan appears to have been insufficient to re-establish the business properly. One can well understand, however, the need for the Corporation to hold fast to certain rules and preconditions, since otherwise they would be faced with an overwhelming number of claims and would have no criteria by which to select those businesses which were to receive assistance.

As in previous cases, it must be accepted that if Abdul Matin is finally forced to dispose of the business, this will not actually deprive society of the productive assets involved. Whoever buys the land, buildings and equipment will presumably do so because he wants to use them productively, and will be able to start the business without the burden of debt which is preventing Matin from recovering.

Matin cannot, however, in any way be blamed for what has happened to his business. His earlier performance suggests that he is very well qualified to continue to own and manage his enterprise, and he has not in any way disqualified himself by withdrawing excessive money for his own use or other forms of financial mismanagement. The total amount owing is not very large, and it should be well within the capacity of the enterprise to earn enough profits to enable Matin to repay what is owing, as well as whatever amount of additional money is necessary in order to re-establish the business on a sound basis. The Corporation should not write off the loan, but should reschedule it on a long term basis and should support Abdul Matin in his efforts to re-build his business and thus to play some part in rebuilding his country.

PASHA'S MACHINE SHOP PROPOSAL, PAKISTAN

The small enterprise sector is believed to employ some three-quarters of the total manufacturing labour force in Pakistan and to have generated some 15% of the country's exports. In recent years there has been little or no net expansion in public or private sector investment in large-scale industries, and they have at times even declined, but small enterprises have continued to grow throughout. In the Province of The Punjab, for instance, it was estimated that investment during the early years of the 1970s in small enterprises was growing at a rate of nearly 15% per year.

Large numbers of people from Pakistan have taken jobs in Western Europe and elsewhere, and many of them obtain both skills and capital with which they can return to Pakistan and start a business of their own. The Government is naturally keen to encourage this, since people of this sort increase the skills available in the country and create employment for others by investing in productive enterprises, rather than buying land and having no effect other than to increase the price of property.

Mr. Pasha spent most of his life in West Germany, working in the textile industry, and in 1977 he decided to return home and to invest his savings in an industrial venture in his own country. He bought a house in Lahore and also bought a car and two truck chassis with him from Germany, in order to start a transport business in addition to his proposed garment factory.

Mr. Pasha knew little or nothing about Pakistan and needed guidance on the necessary procedures involved in importing machinery, on finding land in Lahore for his factory and on how to obtain a loan to buy the land and construct a building. He made some inquiries amongst his friends and relatives and eventually found out that he should approach the Advisory Service of the Punjab Small Industries Corporation. He called on them and they explained that the Small Industries Corporation had made arrangements with a consortium of five commercial banks. The Corporation was responsible for appraising the economic and technical feasibility of proposed investments while one of the banks would assess their credit worthiness. Both the Corporation and the bank would be jointly responsible for any bad debts and a separate reserve fund of 1% of the interest charges was set aside for this purpose. The banks agreed to rule on the credit worthiness of applicants within 15 days of receiving a request from the Corporation; after the funds had been disbursed the Corporation was responsible for monitoring the utilisation of the loan.

The staff of the Advisory Service advised Mr. Pasha to make a loan application. They explained that it would take not less than four months for the Corporation to study the project but once it had been found to be feasible they would recommend it to the bank and the loan would be made available fairly quickly. Mr. Pasha was very pleased and within a few days he submitted an application for a garment factory. He also ordered the necessary machinery from a foreign manufacturer.

In order to save time the Corporation submitted an application to the bank for a ruling on Mr. Pasha's credit worthiness at the same time as they carried out their investigation into the viability of the venture. Because the bank had to make inquiries through their foreign branch, it took four months for them to decide whether or not they would extend a loan to Mr. Pasha. In the meantime, the machinery supplier notified him that the equipment would soon be on its way and he became somewhat worried that he would not have the finance in time to be able to pay for it.

The Corporation completed their study in one month and the recommendation for approval was placed in front of their Committee. Mr. Pasha was invited to attend the meeting and he was delighted that his case was approved; it was then sent to the bank. The bank, however, had not yet approved his credit worthiness and the Corporation was unable to do anything because of the delay. At a further meeting of the Loan Committee, some two months later, the Bank Manager excused the delay by saying that it had been necessary to forward the application to head office because it was for over $20,000. Finally, some six months after his original application, the bank approved Mr. Pasha's project but he had in the meantime returned to Germany and had authorised his cousin to pursue the case on his behalf.

At this stage the Corporation had to refer the application to the Investment Promotion and Supply Division of the Federal Government since it involved imported machinery. Some two months later this Division finally approved the project but the bank was unable finally to sanction the loan because of delays in locating a suitable plot.

The staff of the Corporation had been trying to find a suitable plot in the Lahore Small Industries Estate and they had identified three tenants on the Estate who were in default with their rent. They had been allocated plots a year or more before but had failed to occupy them within six months as their lease agreement had stipulated. Quit notices were therefore issued, in order to release the plots for

Mr. Pasha and other prospective tenants, but the existing tenants appealed to the Industries Department of the Government, and then to a civil court; they finally succeeded in obtaining a temporary injunction against the Corporation and refused to give up their plots.

Mr. Pasha was still in Germany but his cousin had attempted to keep him informed of the various developments. The machinery suppliers were becoming impatient since the equipment had been packed ready for despatch for some months but they had still received no notification that the funds were available. When Mr. Pasha told them about the injunction they said that they could wait no longer and they disposed of the equipment elsewhere. Mr. Pasha felt that he could hardly quarrel with their decision and in any case he was thoroughly disillusioned by all the delays he had suffered. He wrote his cousin and asked him to inform the Corporation and the bank that he was no longer interested in his venture and had decided to stay in Germany.

Comment

The main constraint to new small enterprise in many countries is often not the lack of opportunities, of finance or of individuals with the necessary skills and initiative, but the lengthy procedures and formalities which have to be gone through in order to obtain the necessary licences, finance and other resources. This is a very typical example; Mr. Pasha had the necessary skills and financial stake, and he also had many years of experience working in an industrialized economy which would enable him to make a substantial improvement to the standard of industrial operation in Pakistan. As a result of the bureaucratic problems, he was eventually discouraged from starting an enterprise at all. High level pronouncements of support for new enterprise, or of the welcome which is extended to returning guest workers like Mr. Pasha, are of no value whatsoever, and are worse than useless even if they are not backed up by effective operation of the institutions which must actually carry out the necessary procedures.

Much of the difficulty in this and many similar cases arose from the fact that responsibility for approving the project was divided between the bank and the promotional organization. Banks are naturally unwilling to lend money to finance ventures which they have not investigated, but they also lack the time and the necessary staff to investigate prospective ventures, and the entrepreneurs, in sufficient detail. As a result, both organizations became involved in the appraisal, but neither was able to do the complete job, and the proposal thus fell between the two. The situation was further complicated by the necessity to refer to head office for approval of what does not seem to be a very large sum, and also by the involvement of yet another organization because of the use of foreign equipment.

The problem may arise in part from the involvement of Government; if commercial financing institutions were allowed to compete with one another to finance what appears to be a viable enterprise, where the entrepreneur has a significant stake of his own, there would be unlikely to be such delays since any institution which took as long as those involved in the case study would stand no chance of making a deal with the entrepreneur. People such as Mr. Pasha require little technical or managerial guidance; what they need is a rapid and efficient service to give them the necessary information and back up finance. It is arguable that this is best provided by independent financial institutions and even by consultants, rather than by subsidized Government organizations which may save the entrepreneur some money but whose bureaucratic methods of operation are more likely to frustrate the investment altogether.

PAULOS' SHOE FACTORY, ETHIOPIA

Paulos' family had for many years been involved in the leather business in Addis Ababa, the capital city of Ethiopia. Paulos decided to branch out on his own and in 1960 he started a shoe repair business, employing himself and five of his relatives. They all had some experience in shoe repair, and their business was immediately successful. Their customers soon asked them to manufacture new shoes as well, and by 1968 they had stopped doing repairs altogether. The high quality of their shoes, together with the relative absence of competition helped Paulos to expand the business and he had by this time over 25 employees.

In 1973 Paulos decided further to expand and modernize the factory. He applied for a loan of $15,000 from the Agricultural and Industrial Development Bank, to be repaid over four years. This was approved and the construction of the extension to the building was completed more or less on time. There were some delays in the purchase and importation of the necessary machinery and equipment, and the complete new facility was only fully operational in June 1975.

In 1974, however, the Popular Mass Revolution had broken out in Ethiopia. This brought a number of problems to Paulos' shoe business. First of all it became increasingly difficult to obtain the foreign exchange which was necessary to buy imported raw material. Before the revolution his European suppliers had been willing to sell him the necessary raw materials on six months' credit, but in 1975 they withdrew this facility because of the uncertainty of the political and economic situation in Ethiopia.

Even if it had been possible to obtain the raw materials, it became increasingly difficult to transport goods from the ports to Addis Ababa, which is several hundred kilometres from the sea. Armed forces opposed to the revolution were disrupting communications and the Ethiopian troops were fighting enemies both within and outside the country. As a result military supplies were given priority and Paulos' raw materials could not be brought up to Addis Ababa. Because of the general disruption there was also a shortage of processed hides in the country at the time, and the production and sales revenue dropped alarmingly.

The revolution was inspired by Marxist principles and had therefore strengthened the position of the workers and trade unions.

Paulos' employees had joined a trade union, and he was therefore unable to dismiss any of them, although he did not have enough raw material to keep them busy. Because of his problems he stopped repaying his loan in 1976, and also failed to pay the $5,000 he owed in taxes to the Internal Revenue Service. Early in 1977 the authorities threatened to foreclose and to sell off the assets of Paulos' business, in order to recover the money owing for the loan repayments and taxes. The Government had recently established the Handicraft and Small Industries Development Agency to help craftsmen and small-scale enterprises in the country, and Paulos approached the newly established institution for help.

The Agency's staff investigated Paulos' situation and they were able fairly quickly to arrange for foreign exchange to be made available to him for importing raw materials, and to allocate transport so that goods could reach him from the sea. Their assistance came too late, however; the business had run out of money and Paulos was unable to make use of the facilities they had given him. By this time he was employing over 60 people; Paulos was facing bankruptcy, and they would all lose their jobs.

The staff from the Agency made further investigations and discovered that the factory and equipment were well planned and should be capable of earning substantial profits. There was a large demand for shoes of the quality that Paulos could make, and there was no doubt that Paulos could sell everything he produced, if he had sufficient working capital. They also found out that Paulos still had a general trade licence for imports and export business, as well as his shoe business, and he apparently preferred to devote his time, and what money he had, to general trading than to the shoe factory.

The Agency's main responsibility was to promote employment in small industries in the country, and they therefore recommended that the bank should reschedule the repayment of the remainder of the loan. They suggested that the Internal Revenue should write off all taxes owed by Paulos' Shoe Factory, but they also said that his general import/export trade licence should be withdrawn. They proposed that the local tanneries, which had recently been nationalized, should give Paulos' business priority in supplies of leather, so that he could use his equipment to its full capacity, save imports and generate jobs for the people.

Comment

This enterprise was originally started and subsequently flourished in a traditional free enterprise economy. It was then very seriously affected by the disruption resulting from the Marxist inspired

Revolution in Ethiopia, and it is interesting to see how the authorities reacted to the problems of a fundamentally capitalist enterprise in the new set of circumstances.

They appear to have taken a refreshingly undoctrinaire approach; they have appreciated that the enterprise was already saving foreign exchange by producing goods which would otherwise have to be imported, and was also providing employment to a substantial number of people. They have proposed a set of remedies for its problems which should both enable the business to recover its previous level of activity and also motivate its owner to make a still greater contribution to national development. If their recommendations are accepted, and Paulos plays his part, the enterprise will use fewer imported raw materials and Paulos himself will devote his full attention to expanding its activities and profits.

Many of the comments on the enterprises described in this book imply that Government should not 'bail out' entrepreneurs who have fallen on evil times. In this case, however, the problems cannot in any sense be said to have arisen through Paulos' inefficiency or bad management. He is certainly not to blame for the disruption caused by the Revolution, and it is not usually possible to insure against losses of this sort. The Government, as the ultimate guardian of law and order, is right to accept the responsibility for what has happened and to propose rescheduling of the loan and cancellation of the overdue taxes. This apparent generosity is to be matched by the withdrawal of import privileges. If the national situation becomes stable, and there appears to be a place for individual entrepreneurs such as Paulos in the economy, he is likely to respond to the situation by enthusiastically rebuilding his enterprise and thus contributing to the well being of the nation as a whole.

POPULAR GARMENTS, INDIA

Before the partition of India in 1947 Shyam Lal ran a small cloth shop in Lahore. At partition, like so many millions of other people, he was forced to flee from his home and settled as a refugee in Delhi. He had no money, but he was a skilled tailor, so he took a job in a tailor's shop.

After working for three years he decided to start up on his own. He had saved a small amount of money and bought a sewing machine, and started his business on the pavement, making up clothing from cloth which customers brought to him. He was married, with four children, and was anxious to be able to develop a business in order to support them in the way he wished. He realized that Delhi was growing very fast and that there were therefore many opportunities for anybody who was willing to work hard and to make things that people needed.

The Indian Government had a scheme for rehabilitating refugees such as himself, and in 1956 Shyam Lal was allocated a shop under this scheme. Here he was able to start his business properly; he bought three more sewing machines and employed four tailors. He carried on until 1966 making up clothing to customers' own specifications, and during this time he was able to save about $10,000 because he lived very modestly and only withdrew the absolute minimum for his own expenses. In 1966 Shyam Lal used his savings to buy a shed in the Okhla Industrial Estate which had been set up by the Government for entrepreneurs such as himself.

After studying the market Shyam Lal decided that ready-made garments were now becoming very popular. He borrowed $15,000 from the bank and bought 30 sewing machines and presses; he also had some money left over for working capital to finance raw materials and wages. Within six months he was employing 40 people and had christened his business Popular Garments, specializing in children's clothing, school uniforms and ladies' dresses. He brought in one of his sons as a partner and had no difficulty in selling his products because they were of good quality and there was a substantial demand. By 1972 his business was achieving annual sales of around $100,000 and he had been able to repay the whole of the bank loan as well as to earn a substantial profit. After 1973 business became more difficult because a large number of ready-made garment factories had started in and around Delhi. Profits fell since it was necessary to sell his stocks at cut prices in order to dispose of them. Shyam Lal carried on for two years and then decided that he should try exporting since he had heard that Indian clothing was becoming very popular in the United States and Europe. Garments made from cheesecloth, which could be obtained very cheaply in South India and is very simple to make up, were in great demand in the West and could be sold at a high profit.

In 1976 Shyam Lal succeeded in obtaining an order for $100,000 worth of clothing from the United States. On the strength of this order he was able to borrow $100,000 from the bank in order to finance the production of this order and to purchase some more modern sewing and embroidery machines. The business recovered its earlier prosperity and ever since then the sales have increased every year.

During 1982 Popular Garments sold $300,000 worth of exports and home sales had dwindled to under $5,000. The gross margin, after deducting the cost of labour and materials, was nearly $50,000, and the Government export incentive payments amounted to a further $20,000 during the year. Shyam Lal was thus able to pay the heavy bank interest charges, amounting to over $20,000, and to pay himself a salary of more than $10,000 during the year. He could still re-invest $5,000 in the business after paying all the other expenses.

By the end of the year there was about $400,000 invested in the business. Shyam Lal was well established by this time, and his suppliers were extending credit to a total of $250,000; his bank loans came to a further $125,000, and he had himself reinvested $15,000 from the profits of the business, in addition to his original stake of $10,000.

He appreciated that his suppliers and the banks were together financing over 90% of his investment, but he realized that they too were satisfied with the results, in terms of their profitable sales of material to Popular Garments, and, for the banks, the interest payments they received.

Competition was now increasing in export markets as well, and some of Popular Garments' customers started to complain about the quality of the clothing they were receiving. It appeared that a number of more recently established competitors to Popular Garments had installed imported equipment, from Japan, Germany and the United Kingdom, and this equipment produced better quality garments than the local machinery which Shyam Lal had been able to purchase. He therefore decided to import some similar machines and found out that it would cost $70,000 to purchase 30 of them, along with two embroidering machines; one of his banks offered to finance the transaction.

Shyam Lal, however, was not sufficiently confident to make this investment without a more secure base in the home market. Popular Garments had no retail outlets in Delhi or elsewhere in the country, and Shyam Lal decided to see whether Government institutions, or co-operatives, would be able to help him. He felt that unless he could achieve local sales of around $200,000 a year, to balance his export business, his whole modernization scheme might not be viable. He approached the Government Departments of Industry and Co-operatives, to see whether they would be willing to arrange for his products to be marketed through consumer co-operatives or the Government emporia. They promised to examine his request.

Comment

Shyam Lal is a typical example of a refugee who, like so many before him, lost everything he had and started again in an alien environment, with great success. From the very beginning, he looked objectively at the opportunities that were available and made the best use of his skills, and eventually the money he was able to save, in order to build a successful business.

He benefitted on numerous critical occasions from support from Government and from the banks. It is significant that the initiative, and the initial investment, came from himself. He took advantage of Government schemes to provide premises and finance, but did not need any advice or assistance in terms of management or product policy. Assistance was available, when he needed it, and he was able to make use of it reasonably quickly.

When Shyam Lal met competition, first in garments made to customers' specifications, then in the home market and latterly in export markets, he was willing to make fundamental changes in the nature of his business in order to overcome the problems. He did not, however, receive any special facilities from Government or the banks which were not available to people of the same initiative and ability as himself. It might be argued that his success so far suggests that it would be unnecessary for Government to offer him the special marketing assistance he is requesting. If Government guarantees the market for an enterprise, without reference to quality or prices, it is performing a dis-service to the consumers and, eventually, to the business as well. Without the stimulus of competition no business can remain a leader in its field, and Shyam Lal could probably develop his own local sales without special preferential treatment.

By normal standards, the business is relying excessively on banks and suppliers for its finance, and Shyam Lal himself has a very small stake in it. Both the banks and the suppliers are presumably confident of the viability of the business, and if the bank finance is on purely commercial terms, with no element of subsidy, there is presumably no reason why they should not carry on extending credit in this way. If the bank's funds are scarce, however, and are intended to assist new smaller enterprises, it could be that the bank should give greater preference to entrepreneurs at an earlier stage in their business, with a greater relative commitment, like Shyam Lal at the beginning of his own business.

PRAMOD AND THE DISTRICT INDUSTRIAL CENTRE, INDIA

Pramod was a semi-skilled mechanic who had worked in various factories in the city of Calcutta. He then returned to his home town and worked for some time in a co-operative firm which manufactured aluminium utensils. He eventually became foreman of this factory and was effectively its manager; he studied both the commercial and the technical aspects of the operation at close quarters and gained a great deal of experience in this way.

After working in this factory for two years he decided to launch his own factory, albeit on a very modest scale at the outset. He approached the local bank for a loan in order to buy a lathe to spin the circular utensils and some dyes to colour them, and for working capital to buy raw materials and to finance his stocks of finished goods. Pramod himself had no finance and since the bank required guarantors in this case he persuaded his brother and his brother-in-law, who was an employee of the Electricity Department, to be joint guarantors. The bank made him a loan of $2,000 on this basis, and Pramod purchased the machine and raw materials and went into production.

For about six months everything went according to plan; he sold all the goods he manufactured and made the scheduled loan repayments as they fell due. Then, however, things went wrong and the bank found that he had stopped making his repayments. They approached the guarantors but they were unwilling to lend him any more money and the sales of the unit fell off since Pramod was running out of working capital.

At about the same time the Government opened a District Industries Centre in the town, and carried out extensive publicity to inform industrialists in the area of their wide range of services. The Government of India had in fact introduced District Industries Centres to provide a 'one stop service' for business people and to avoid the problems which arose from their having to make contact with large numbers of different institutions, whose policies and decisions might not be co-ordinated with one another.

Pramod heard about the Centre and made an appointment to meet the General Manager. They had an interesting discussion and Pramod asked for his assistance. The General Manager was delighted to help; he discussed the problem with a senior staff member from the regional office of the bank which had financed Pramod's venture and together with this man he visited the local branch which had provided the finance. He also visited the factory itself along with representatives from the bank.

The Manager, as well as the people from the bank, gained the impression that Pramod was an excellent worker and that there was a promising market for his products. They decided to assist Pramod to revive the factory and therefore asked him to explain the problems which had prevented him from keeping up with his loan repayments.

Pramod gave a lengthy account of his problems; it appeared that his brother and his brother-in-law, who were his guarantors, wanted to share in the profits of the business even though they had never made any agreement to do this at the beginning. As a result they had withdrawn money from the business and there had not been enough working capital to buy further dyes and other material, nor had it been possible to make repayments to the bank on time. He had left most of the commercial operations to his brother and his brother-in-law; they had carried out the sales but had then retained the money they received rather than crediting it against his loan account.

The Manager of the District Industries Centre was then all the more convinced that they should support Pramod but the bankers disagreed. They felt that Pramod was a wilful defaulter and the guarantors supported them in this conclusion; they said that Pramod had spent more than he earned and that they could not therefore trust him with any additional funds. After several rounds of discussion with the Bank Manager, the guarantors and staff from the regional office of the bank, the Manager of the District Industries Centre succeeded in persuading the various parties to agree to the following scheme in order to revive the factory. They would convert the existing working capital loan into a term loan, rescheduling the payments accordingly, and would then issue a new working capital loan to allow Pramod to operate at a higher level of business. The guarantors agreed to guarantee this loan, and, together with Pramod, to invest money of their own to increase the owners's stake in the business. The Manager of the Centre and the bank staff agreed to work together to supervise the account and to help Pramod to revive his business.

The Manager of the local branch of the bank prepared a paper outlining the proposal and sent it to his regional office. After some time the regional office returned the proposal to the branch on the basis of a small technical error in the calculations, although the proposal had in fact originally been drawn up by a staff member of the regional office when he visited the branch. The General Manager of the District Industries Centre found out about it and was very annoyed. He immediately took the matter up with the local

Branch Manager who in turn complained to his regional office and promised to correct the proposal and to resubmit it. The Manager of the District Industries Centre also brought the matter up in a regular co-ordination meeting with the bank and suggested that cases of this sort should be solved by amicable discussion across the table rather than through correspondence and memoranda.

More than a year went by; although the Manager at the Centre and the local Branch Manager continually pressed the regional office of the bank they failed to make a decision on the proposal. The Manager of the Centre felt that his credibility was at stake, and the local Branch Manager was reluctant to press the case too vigorously since he was after all disagreeing with his own superiors. Pramod himself was not sure whether or not to continue trying to obtain new finance through the District Industries Centre and the bank. A number of the older business people in the area suggested that he should sell his equipment and become their employee. The Board of the co-operative where he used to work also asked him to come back and to work for them again, at a higher salary, and Pramod wondered whether he should give up his dream of becoming the owner of a factory and instead spend the rest of his life as an employee of others.

Comment

Yet again, problems appear to have arisen because of lack of co-ordination between and within financing institutions, in spite of the fact that the Government set up a special Centre in order to avoid exactly such problems. In the beginning, when only Pramod and the bank were involved, he obtained his loan without too much difficulty and was able to start his enterprise. When things went wrong, because of personal problems, misunderstanding and disagreement between him and his guarantors, his approach to the new District Industries Centre appears actually to have been a mistake. The Manager of the Centre made every effort to overcome the problems, by working formally and informally with staff of the branch and the regional office of the bank, but all to no avail. Because Pramod was relying on their assistance, he appears to have made no other efforts to solve the problem. The business has operated at a very low level, or has been entirely closed, for many months, and its recovery is likely to be all the more difficult for that. As so often happens, a delayed decision has probably caused more difficulty than a prompt negative decision might have done.

In spite of the best efforts of the Manager of the Centre, it appears that the involvement of yet another institution, even one whose objective is to improve co-ordination, has only made things worse. If the local Branch Manager had had the authority to make decisions on his own it is possible that he would have been able to reach a similar agreement with Pramod and his guarantors, and to revive the unit and recover his loan at the same time. Problems arose because of the need to refer to the regional office, and it may be that their staff felt it necessary to demonstrate their independence and resented the intervention of the District Industries Centre which they regarded as an upstart organization which was attempting to come between them and their clients. The local Branch Manager should certainly have explained the position clearly to the guarantors at the very beginning, in order to avoid the type of mis-understanding that arose. As things are, however, Pramod might be well advised to inform the local Branch Manager of his intention to sell his equipment, pay off the loan and become an employee once again. This threat may encourage the guarantors and the bank to make a decision. If Pramod does sell the equipment it will not be lost to the economy but will presumably be operated by somebody else; it should be appreciated that a transfer of assets does not necessarily mean a loss to the community.

THE RETLADIRA WELDING WORKS, SOUTH AFRICA

M. J. Gomba was a skilled worker who was employed in a factory near Pretoria in South Africa, manufacturing bodies for motor vehicles. Around 1975 he decided to go into business on his own; he bought a small electric arc-welder and started to make security bars to protect houses against burglars, initially on a part-time basis.

Because the law in South Africa forbids Africans from operating businesses except in the so-called 'homelands', which are a long way from the major markets and from sources of raw materials, he had to operate in his back yard. Nevertheless, there was a tremendous demand for his products, and after three months he gave up his job at the vehicle company and also had to hire three more people to help him. He was soon able to buy a second-hand delivery van and by 1979 his business had done so well that he was able to buy a brand new vehicle with which he could collect steel and deliver his products to the sites where they were to be installed.

By this time he had added window frames, iron fences and gates, portable corrugated iron shelters, shelving and vehicle bodies to his product range, and it became obvious that he could no longer continue to operate from behind his house. He realized that he would have to obtain proper premises, even though this would mean moving to his tribal 'homeland', which was some 30 kilometres away from where he started. He knew that it would in many ways be more difficult to operate his business at such a distance from his customers and his suppliers, but he concluded that the advantages of a legal location outweighed the advantages of continuing to operate where he was. He could not expand his business in his back yard, and because it was illegal he could not advertise or even arrange for his larger suppliers to deliver raw material to him. If he wished to borrow money from the bank, he could not use the place where he lived as security, both because he had no right to operate a factory there and in any case he had no title deeds. In South Africa, Africans are not permitted to own land in the townships where they are allowed to reside on a temporary basis, and, although a system of lease-hold tenure had recently been introduced, this was only for residential and not for industrial purposes.

Mr. Gomba therefore set about to obtain a licence. This was not easy because there were lengthy procedures which had to be gone

A carpenter with a traditional bow saw, in Africa.

Partners in a watch repair business in Northern India.

A tinsmith under a mango tree by Lake Malawi.

through, and although he managed to obtain a site in his 'homeland', he could not obtain the freehold to this either, since it was 'tribal trust land' which was under the jurisdiction of the Chief and could not be used as security for loans. He knew that when his business was licensed he would have to keep accounts, and pay taxes, but he realized that this was the only way in which to expand and he therefore made the necessary application.

He eventually succeeded in obtaining his licence in 1982 and started to build a factory – the Retladira Welding Works – on the site which had been allocated to him by the Chief. He invested his savings of $56,000 in the building and eventually moved his operation to the new location in the middle of 1983. He still employed his three full-time labourers and his sales were by this time running at around $3,000 a month. He was paying himself a salary of $600 a month, and each of his workers was receiving $200; this was rather higher than the normal prevailing industrial wage. He had about $6,000 worth of equipment, in addition to his vehicles which were worth about $5,000, and he also had around $5,000 in the bank. When his stocks of raw materials and partially finished work were included, the total of all his assets was almost $18,000. He had financed all this from his initial savings and subsequent earnings, without having borrowed anything from the bank or elsewhere.

Although his business has succeeded very well, and is enabling him to earn a great deal more money than he was previously paid, he still has a number of problems. In South Africa it is very difficult for Africans to sell to, or even to buy from, large non-African businesses. Even if Mr. Gomba can find a Purchasing Manager who is willing to deal with him, the social barriers make it very difficult to form any lasting business relationships, and Mr. Gomba's education is such that he finds it hard to follow the procedures necessary for formal tendering, invoicing and so on. Even if he could bring his production up to the specifications demanded by the South African Bureau of Standards, which is unlikely, he would find it very hard to get their official approval. In any case, he faces very severe competition from larger non-African businesses which are able to buy material in greater quantities, and thus less expensively, and can manufacture their goods on automatic machinery at less expense and to closer standards.

Mr Gomba thus has to rely largely on the African market but this too has its problems. Africans in South Africa have come to believe that products made by their own people are necessarily of a lower standard than those which come from large, internationally known companies. Those Africans who are relatively fortunate and are earning quite good wages with big companies, living in the townships outside the 'homelands', are unable to invest their money in freehold property. As a result they are very keen on modern gadgets and Mr. Gomba is unable to manufacture self-opening gates or other more sophisticated variants of his products which require modern development departments and knowledge of skills other than welding.

The people living around his factory in the 'homeland' are generally very poor. Only a very few of them commute to jobs outside the 'homeland', and most of them depend on subsistence farming for their livelihood. During the drought seasons many of them are near to starvation. They therefore offer very little of a market for the products of the Retladira Welding Works, and Mr. Gomba would very much prefer to be able to locate his business in one of the townships. A few small factories are now being made available to African entrepreneurs in the townships, but there is a great demand for them and only people with good connections can succeed in obtaining one.

Comment

At first sight most of the problems of the Retladira Welding Works appear to arise from the racialist policies of South Africa. He cannot borrow money from a bank because there are few opportunities for Africans to obtain freehold land, he has limited management skill because the bulk of educational resources are reserved for non-Africans and he finds it difficult to do business with large companies because of the social barriers between the races in South Africa.

Difficulties of this sort are particularly blatant and obvious in South Africa, because many of the barriers between the races are enforced by law. They are, however, very similar to the informal barriers which exist between economic groups in other developing countries. Rural entrepreneurs have no security for bank finance, and squatters in urban slum areas are no better off. The elite enjoy far better education than the vast mass of the poor, and similar barriers exist between the managers of large local or multi-national enterprises and small-scale entrepreneurs, even when they are from the same racial group.

In spite of these problems, the Retladira Welding Works is a successful enterprise. Mr. Gomba probably regrets the political system under which he has to operate, and may very rightly devote some of his time and his money to try to change it. Nevertheless, as far as his business is concerned, he has to make the best of the situation as he finds it. He has apparently succeeded so far by offering a personal service and tailor made products for specific applications, where the lack of standardization and more labour intensive methods are unlikely to be a disadvantage. He should continue to specialize in this way, rather then attempting to compete with larger businesses, and will thus in the long term contribute to the growing wealth, political awareness and eventual liberation of his people.

THE RITA FOOD COMPANY, MALAYSIA

The Government of Malaysia has always promoted the establishment of local small enterprises, both because of their general contribution to economic development and because they provide a means whereby the 'Bumi Putra', or indigenous people, can increase their participation in the economy. A whole array of financing, training and other forms of promotional assistance is now available to entrepreneurs, and there are a number of programmes designed to encourage people who retire from Government service or the Army to set up their own businesses.

Mr. Raseed was an ex-Army Officer who had worked for several years in the Supply Division and had gained a good insight into the Army's supply and purchasing procedures. He attended a two week entrepreneurial development course conducted by the Malaysian Ex-Servicemen's Association and the National Productivity Centre, and decided to start the Rita Food Company to manufacture tomato ketchup and soya sauce. He knew that the Government wished to encourage indigenous small enterprises, and he was confident that he would obtain a contract from the Military Supply Division.

Mr. Raseed recruited an ex-employee from a large food company to help him with the arrangements; they produced a plan of operation and applied to a commercial bank for a loan of $10,000 at the special subsidized interest rate of 7%. This was approved and he set up his manufacturing facilities accordingly.

Mr. Raseed bid for a number of Army and other Government contracts for the supply of tomato ketchup and soya sauce. His bids to supply tomato ketchup were unsuccessful, because his product did not meet the specifications laid down by the National Standards Organization. He was, however, successful in obtaining a contract to supply soya sauce to three universities.

The previous supplier of soya sauce had been the Royal Food Company, which was an indigenous company with wide interests in a range of food products. This Company was also a major supplier of the special yeast which has to be used when making soya sauce. The Rita Food Company bought its yeast from Royal Food, but were at this point notified that they would have to seek an alternative supplier. Mr. Raseed knew that if he could not obtain enough yeast he would not be able to manufacture soya sauce and he contacted as many of his competitors as he could in order to find alternative sources of supply. He found that almost all of them obtained their yeast from Royal Food as he did. Fortunately, the owner of one small factory agreed to sell some of his yeast to Rita Food and this was enough to enable Mr. Raseed to meet his delivery schedules for the next three months.

In the meantime Mr. Raseed received a number of complaints from the universities about the soya sauce. The students had found foreign material in the sauce and the universities were naturally very concerned. Mr. Raseed asked for advice about the problem from an Industrial Extension Officer; he recommended that the bottles should be washed and filled by machine rather than by hand but Mr. Raseed was unable to follow the advice because the cheapest automatic washing and filling machine cost $8,000.

One of the universities then notified the Rita Food Company that it would cancel its contract if the next batch of soya sauce contained any foreign material. The Industrial Extension Officer examined the problem in more detail and pointed out that Mr. Raseed's Company also suffered from a variety of other problems such as bad marketing organization, poor management, outmoded production techniques and poor product quality. In addition, the Company's Accountant produced some figures for the first six months of operation which showed that the Rita Company had lost money throughout the period.

Businesses employing five or less people in Malaysia are exempted from certain Government regulations. The Rita Food Company had a total of eight employees and Mr. Raseed had therefore to give his employees paid holidays and maternity leave and allowances. He had in addition to contribute to the Provident and Compensation Funds, and to make social security payments for his employees. As a result of these overheads the Rita Food Company's costs were higher than its smaller competitors, while its scale of operations was insufficient to enable it to compete with the large-scale producers. Mr. Raseed realized that he would have to improve the quality of his products and reduce the costs of operation if his business was to survive.

Comment

People who have retired from military service often make good entrepreneurs. They have learnt how to organize people, to discipline themselves and to work hard, and they have usually accumulated some savings, or retirement benefits. which they can use as their stake in a new enterprise. In a number of countries, people are encouraged to retire early from Government service in order to start their own enterprises, since this contributes to economic activity and also makes room for younger people to enter the Government service. This is a particularly useful strategy in countries where there is a need to correct a racial imbalance in the ownership of enterprise, since the indigenous majority are likely to be well represented in the public service; if they can be encouraged to start new enterprises they will be able to use the skills and resources they have acquired to promote more equitable development.

Mr. Raseed appears, like many in his position, to have believed that his contacts and knowledge of purchasing procedures were the main keys to business success. He drew on outside expertise for the planning of his business, but underestimated the importance of close personal control of quality and production. He relied entirely on public sector contracts for his sales. This meant that he did not have to have any marketing or sales organization, but it did make him dependent on one or two customers, and sales of this kind are usually made at lower prices than sales through normal retail channels. It was natural that Mr. Raseed should seek business of this sort, because of his previous contacts, but it meant that he had to fulfil his contracts at whatever cost. If his sales had been spread over a large number of smaller accounts, he might have been able to cut production rather than have to buy yeast at an inflated price.

Small-scale business people commonly complain about Government regulations and contributions, and Rita Food Company certainly seems to have fallen into a difficult gap, since its number of employees was just above the maximum to qualify for exemption from social security contributions and so on. Government might be advised to consider a graduated scale of contributions, depending on the size of enterprise, but any change of this sort might involve added complexity and expensive administration which would more than outweigh its benefits.

Mr. Raseed should be encouraged not to rely too much on the various programmes of assistance, advice and training which are available for indigenous entrepreneurs. The future of his business lies in his own hands. He should probably spend more time personally supervizing the production operation, and should also attempt to diversify his outlets by selling through normal wholesale and retail channels. If he loses some of his contract business, this may mean that he has to reduce the scale of his operation, but this need not necessarily be a bad thing, particularly if it would bring down the number of his employees to a level at which he qualifies for exemption from the various contributions to Government funds.

ST. PATRICKS SEWING CO-OPERATIVE, DOMINICA

St. Patricks is a village about 40 kilometres from Roseau, the capital of the island of Dominica in the Caribbean. The population of the whole country is under 100,000, and St. Patricks and the neighbouring villages have a total population of around 4,000. The people's houses are fairly distant from one another, and the whole area of St. Patricks is rather cut off from the rest of the island. The local people do not travel into Roseau very often, since the cost of the bus trip is rather expensive.

There are only a few shops in St. Patricks and the surrounding villages, and they stock only basic foodstuffs and household goods. A few travelling traders come to the area, selling clothing and fabrics, but when people need to buy anything special they travel into Roseau. There is thus very little contact between the people in the area, and their only regular meeting places are at the banana boxing plant every Thursday, and at the various local churches on Sunday.

In 1976 a foreign agency made a gift of a number of domestic electric sewing machines to the island. The Department of Local Government was given the task of distributing them to different villages in the country. Communities were asked to put up good proposals as to how they would use a machine, and those who made the best suggestions received one. Although there was no electricity in St. Patricks, the Village Council made a good proposal and were given a sewing machine as a result.

After some discussion the Village Council organized a group of six women to meet on three afternoons and evenings a week in order to teach the young girls in the village how to sew. They bought two old manual machines and converted the new electric machine to treadle operation. They met in the building of the local farming co-operative, without paying any rent, and they organized fund raising events in order to obtain money to buy fabric, thread, zip fasteners and so on. Three of the six women who were responsible for the training already had sewing machines of their own and were already in business for themselves, making clothing, curtains, pillow cases and so on to order for local people. The number of pupils who came to learn how to sew with the new group fluctuated, but the enterprise managed to continue and the women sold the clothes that the trainees made so that they could buy more materials.

A Mrs. Joseph was generally acknowledged as the leader of the group and she used to buy fabric for them in Roseau and decide at what price to sell the clothes they made. She had the experience and contacts to enable her to do this because she was one of the three who were already in business on her own account at home. One of the Village Council members kept records for the venture, and early in 1978 they succeeded in obtaining a grant from an international voluntary agency to pay for five of their pupils to be trained in one of the three garment manufacturing businesses in Roseau.

Towards the end of 1978 the six women who had started the venture and were responsible for the training told the Village Council that they were no longer prepared to give their services free of charge. They felt that the Council should arrange for some payment to be made to them, although they said that they did not expect to receive the same wages as they could have earned if they went to work for one of the companies in Roseau.

The Council had no money of its own but they were keen to continue the venture. They knew that one of the other groups which had received a sewing machine had successfully obtained sub-contracts for making overalls and other clothes from the larger garment manufacturers in Roseau. The Council thought that it might be possible to continue their venture by reorganizing it as a money making enterprise as well as keeping up the local training programme. They applied for a grant to the same agency that had paid for five pupils to be trained in Roseau, in order to cover the cost of reorganizing the venture, and to give them more time to consider the problem. They were given a total of $650 and the agency made it clear that they would not be able to provide any further help. The Council gave each of the six women $70 for what they had done, and at that point Mrs. Joseph decided to leave the group.

Early in the next year the local farming co-operative said that they could no longer make their building available for the sewing group. The Village Council then rented a room to the group for $10 a month, and four more pupils were sent to be trained in Roseau, since the other five had now returned to St. Patricks.

After the departure of Mrs. Joseph, nobody really knew how to price the clothes they produced, nor did they know how much she had paid for the fabric. The women who remained, and their pupils, continued to produce clothes from the stocks of materials that had already been bought, and they attempted to price them at more or less the same level as Mrs. Joseph. The prices were somewhat lower than for similar products in Roseau, but the quality and finish of the garments was not always good, and the women acknowledged that there was need for improvement.

Although they succeeded in selling a certain number of garments, it was clear that the group was not self-supporting and that some improvements were needed. The Village Council, and the women, thought that they might start to make school uniforms. The local people preferred to send their children to school in uniforms, and at that time there was only one supplier of the correct coloured fabric. She was a certain Ma Baba, of the Reliance Dress Shop in Roseau, and because she also made up uniforms she was not willing to sell large quantities of the fabric to anyone else. No one knew where she got the fabric from.

The Village Council was not sure how to proceed. They asked their Treasurer to examine the records of the venture in order to help them make a decision. They knew that the Department of Local Government in the island had a loan scheme for small businesses and they thought that they might be able to obtain a loan to help them start a small enterprise in St. Patricks, based on the sewing training venture. The Treasurer presented the following figures:

Income and Expenditure for the St. Patricks Sewing Group, January 1978 to July 1979

Income		$
Fund Raising Events		160
Grant from Voluntary Agency		650
Sales Revenue		900
Total Income		$1,710

Expenditure	$	$
Materials	830	
Wages	420	
Entertainment	60	
Transport	40	
Rent	40	
Other Expenses	70	
Total Expenditure		1,460
Stocks in Hand		
Finished Garments	150	
Materials	100	
Total Stocks		250
Total Expenditure and Stocks		$1,710

Comment

This group was started at the initiative of the local community. They responded to the opportunity of obtaining a sewing machine free of charge, but they themselves had to prepare the proposal and decide what to do with the machine; it was not 'handed to them on a plate'.

From the beginning the venture benefitted from the voluntary services of a number of experienced women, who were sufficiently public spirited to share their skill with young people in the community and not to charge for their services. Above all, they had an experienced leader who was familiar with both the technical and commercial aspects of the business.

The initial objective of the group was to provide sewing training for young people in the community, and this seems to have succeeded fairly well. Not only were girls trained in the village itself, but a number were also sent for more advanced training in the capital city as a result of the group's initiative. It was hardly surprising, however, that after some time the trainers should demand some payment for their services. They presumably realized that they were in fact helping other people to become competitive with themselves, and the group was receiving substantial assistance from outside agencies; they saw no reason why they should continue to give their time for nothing.

Activities which are only viable when a significant portion of the labour is provided free of charge are unlikely to survive for very long. Volunteers are usually willing to give their time in order to start an enterprise, but are less likely to be willing to continue, particularly if they see that other people are making money out of it. It is far better for an enterprise to be started as a result of community goodwill, and to be 'subsidized' in this way in its early years, rather than to be imposed from the outside by Government. In either case, however, the ultimate test is the ability of an enterprise to earn its own keep and it should not have to depend on voluntary work, or on external subsidy, for more than a few years at most.

The results of the leader's departure show how vital effective leadership is for any enterprise. A small business is effectively an extension of the entrepreneur's personality. It is unrealistic to expect a small community enterprise to be any different. If this group is to become a genuinely self-supporting business, it may be possible to re-engage the interest of Mrs. Joseph or another leader on the basis of the profits that can be earned from it. It may be possible to find someone who is willing to work, if not for nothing, for a very low reward because of the social implications of the group, but people of this sort are very few and far between.

The figures that have been made available, although they are far from complete and do not give all the information that would be provided by a simple balance sheet and profit and loss account, do show that the total sales were very little more then the cost of material, and the group was obviously very much dependent on the generosity of outside donors, as well as voluntary labour from the women who helped to start it. It may be that it would be quite impossible to make a viable enterprise out of the group, particularly in view of its remote location, and it would be most unwise to borrow money through the Local Government scheme if this is the case. The group should carefully appraise the future possibilities, preferably with advice from somebody with experience in small enterprise, and they may have to accept that the best solution is for the individual women, and their trainees, to operate on their own – as some of the women are already doing. If there is an economic market for their products, it is probable that one or two of the women will do better than the others, and will be able to offer employment to their fellows. There is no reason why businesses of this sort should not perform just as valuable a social and economic function as the original group which provided the training to make such businesses possible.

THE SIAYA SUGAR COMPANY, KENYA

A number of large-scale sugar mills have, in recent years, been established in western Kenya, and thousands of farmers in the area have greatly increased their incomes by growing sugar cane. The production potential of Siaya District, however, was not sufficient to justify the construction of a large-scale mill, but the area was very suitable for sugar cane, and a number of farmers grew it. They sold their cane to very small local factories which made 'jaggery', used mainly for brewing local beer, but these factories were unable to pay reasonable prices for cane, and there were in any case not enough of them.

A group of three businessmen realized that this offered an opportunity. They knew that technology existed for medium-scale factories, producing around 100,000 tons of sugar a year, and two of them had their own mechanical engineering firm in which they knew they could construct most of the necessary machinery. They would only have to import certain critical pieces of equipment from India.

The three businessmen investigated the proposition in some detail. They decided to set up a nucleus estate on which they would grow about a third of the sugar cane they needed, and they planned to buy the balance from individual out-growers. They proposed to organize a co-operative or other similar institution to act as an intermediary between them and the private farmers. They knew that all sugar of the appropriate standard could be sold to the Kenya National Trading Corporation at a Government controlled price which would allow for a reasonable processing margin after paying for the cane. The Company would not therefore have to set up its own marketing organization, and both its selling and buying prices would be controlled by Government.

The three partners incoporated their business in 1976. They had calculated that a total investment of $467,000 would be required; they were able themselves to contribute cash, land for the mill and the nucleus estate, and the equipment (which was made locally) to a value of $200,000; they then applied to a local development bank for a loan of $267,000 to cover the balance. It took some nine months to process their application, and in the meantime the cost of the imported equipment had gone up by $13,000 while the materials for the machinery which was to be made locally had increased in cost by another $9,000. The development bank allowed the partners to divert part of the money which had been allocated for working capital to cover these increases, and they negotiated with a commercial bank for an overdraft to meet the difference.

Unfortunately, however, the Government imposed a credit squeeze at this time. It therefore proved impossible to obtain an overdraft, and the Company had to start operations with rather less finance than had been planned. In addition, the partners had neglected to provide the land or organize the cultivation of a nucleus estate, because so many farmers had told them how glad they were that they would be able to find an outlet for their cane.

The Company started operations at exactly the right time, when the maximum amount of cane was ready to be harvested. Although the Co-operative had not been formed, a number of farmers responded enthusiastically and the Company was also able to draw from a small stock-pile of cane which had been accumulated during the few days preceding the start of operation. The farmers were paid in cash, and at the end of the first month the partners were delighted to find that sales and profits had exceeded expectations.

The results were almost as good in the second month, but from that point on the Company found it more and more difficult to obtain supplies of cane. Because of their shortage of working capital, they were not able to pay the farmers as promptly as they promised, and some of them had to wait for over three months. In addition, they had not made adequate arrangements for transport. They had initially been able to hire independent contractors, to bring the farmers' cane to the factory, but this cost a great deal of money and in addition the contractors were not willing to wait for their money. By the end of the sixth month, when cane harvesting stopped for the season, the partners were disappointed to find that the business had lost almost $400,000.

During the second season of operations, starting in late 1979, the situation became even more serious. In addition to the need for cash to pay the farmers and the transport contractors, the first instalment on the loan had become due and there seemed to be no way in which it could be paid. Towards the end of the season, early in 1980, the Company managed to borrow another $20,000 from a different bank, to alleviate their working capital situation. This provided some temporary respite, but further increased the Company's burden and they then applied to the original bank to reschedule their repayments. The bankers examined the situation in some detail and concluded that this would not be a solution. They declined the Company's request and advised the partners to set up the nucleus estate as they had originally proposed. If they did this, they said, they would within a year be able to rely entirely on their own estate for sugar cane, and would not have to rely on independent farmers.

The partners realized that this was good advice, but they could not follow it. They were unable to buy the land they would need, nor did they have enough money to plant it with sugar cane. Meanwhile, arrears continued to accumulate and they were declared to be in default early in 1981. Although they had recommended that the Company should rely on a nucleus estate, their bankers realized that by this time a substantial number of farmers had come to depend on the Company as a market for their cane. These people would suffer if the Company closed, or if it succeeded in developing its own estate, and the bankers knew that one of their objectives was to improve the well being of less fortunate members of society, such as small-scale farmers.

Comment

This business seems initially to have had everything in its favour. There was a guaranteed market for its products, a number of small-scale farmers were anxious to supply its raw material, two of the investors had experience in mechanical engineering and the development bank was willing to give generous support because the Company would save foreign exchange and provide a market for large numbers of individual farmers.

There were a number of reasons why things did not turn out as well as expected. As so often happens, no allowance had been made for cost increases while the proposal was being appraised. This led to a reduction in the limited funds that had been allocated to working capital, and this was made more serious because the entrepreneurs had not organized the co-operative or their own nucleus estate as had been proposed.

Although the sugar mill itself was not a very large undertaking, and the partners appear to have been able to manage it effectively when it had an adequate supply of raw material, they failed to appreciate the complexity of the cane supply operation which was really a part of the whole enterprise. It is by no means certain that they would have been able to organize a co-operative, even if they had tried, and the transport is also a substantial operation in its own right, requiring specialized management. The bankers should probably have realized that the investors had indeed identified a good opportunity, but should have ensured that they had access to specialized expertise in the various functions that were involved. The situation can clearly not be allowed to continue. It may be possible for the investors, or somebody else, to raise a mortgage in order to set up a nucleus estate, or there may be a suitable local leader among the farming community who could organize a co-operative which would be able to finance members' production so that they would not require immediate payment from the mill. It might even be possible for such a co-operative actually to take over the mill itself, but if neither of these alternatives is possible, the bankers would be well advised to foreclose and force the investors to dispose of the mill. The equipment has apparently been properly selected and has proved itself capable of producing saleable sugar in the right quantities; all that is necessary is for the cane supply operation to be effectively organized.

THE SIDECO FAN MANUFACTURING VENTURE, INDIA

The Kerala State Small Industries Development and Employment Corporation (SIDECO) was set up to assist small industries in the State of Kerala, in India, to provide various services such as industrial estates, raw material supplies, training and advice. It was also decided that the Corporation should itself actually set up certain enterprises, generally in conjunction with large businesses elsewhere in India, in order to bring new industries to the State and to demonstrate to local entrepreneurs what could be done. As a result, the Corporation now runs 15 small factories, manufacturing items such as furniture, tiles, pottery, industrial tools and iron castings.

In 1977 the management of SIDECO decided to start manufacturing ceiling fans. There was a large demand for these fans in the State, and they were all imported from other parts of India. They therefore entered into a collaboration agreement with one of the leading ceiling fan manufacturing companies in India. Under the agreement, which was to last in the first instance for five years, SIDECO paid an initial lump sum of $15,000 to the fan manufacturer. This was to cover the preparation of a detailed project report for the unit, and for assistance in selecting the site, preparing the plant layout, choosing the plant and machinery, and supervising the pilot production of the initial batches of fans. In addition, SIDECO was to pay royalty of 1% of its sales of fans to the large manufacturer, and the manufacturer in its turn guaranteed to purchase the new unit's production of 50,000 fans per annum for the five year period. The price was to be 14% lower than the price at which the company normally sold its fans to its dealers, to allow a marketing margin. SIDECO was also at liberty to sell fans direct to public sector purchasers in the State of Kerala, and was to pay a 4% additional royalty on such sales to the manufacturer. The manufacturer also accepted a penalty clause, which would be payable if production was delayed unreasonably after the physical facilities had been provided by SIDECO.

The total investment was approximately $600,000. $140,000 was for plant and machinery, $100,000 for land and buildings, $30,000 for pre-operative expenses and the balance for working capital. SIDECO invested approximately $200,000; a group of banks made a term loan of $170,000 and the balance was provided in the form of an overdraft.

Arc welding at a metalworks.

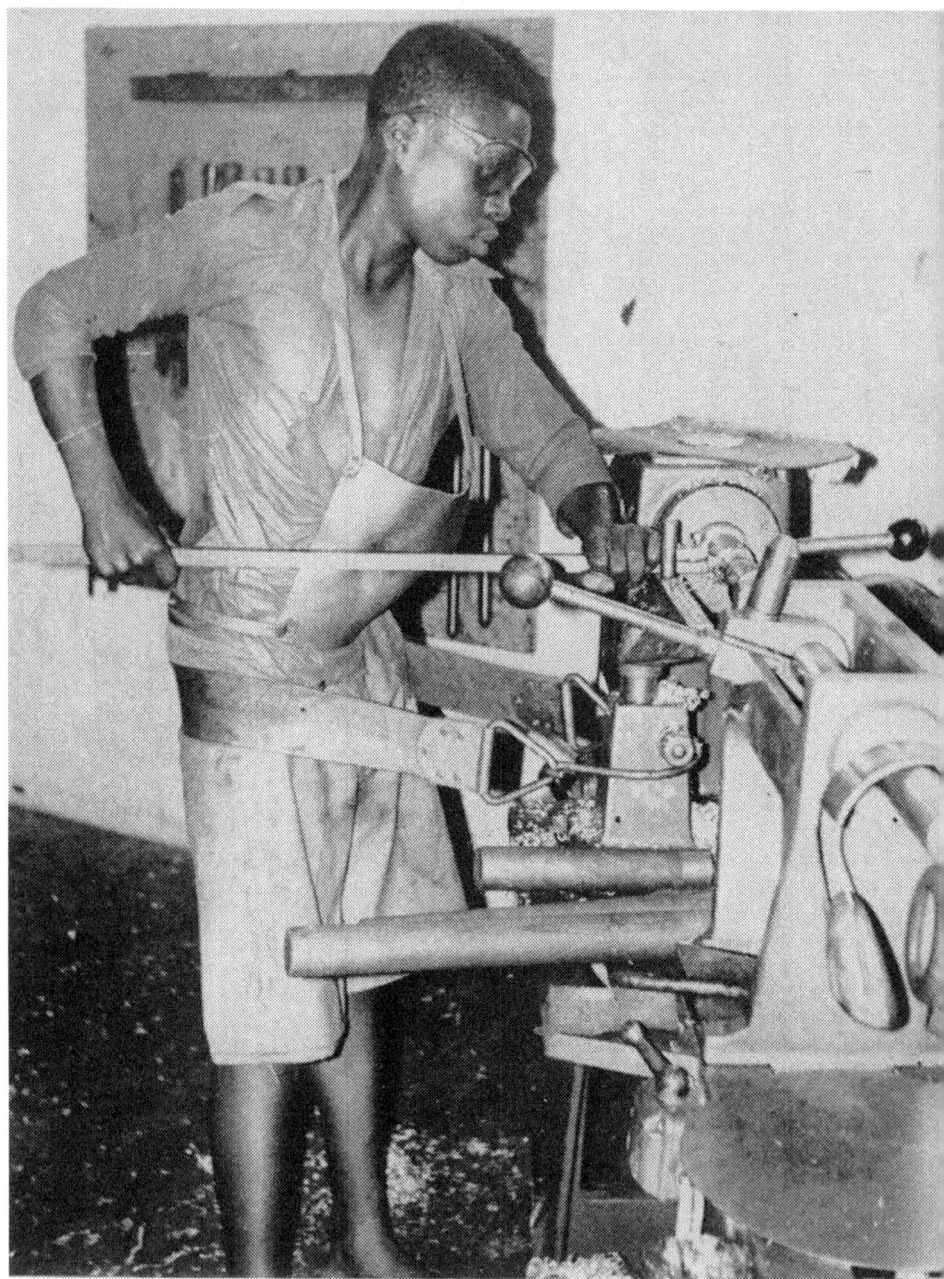

Spinning aluminium pots.

The unit started production some 15 months after the date of signing the agreement; there were some changes from the plan, since only 52 workers were recruited as opposed to the 94 that had been envisaged, and they did not install a die casting section as had been planned. Instead, die castings were purchased from a factory some 200 kilometres away, whose costs were rather higher than those which had been estimated for the new unit, so that each fan cost some 60 cents more than had been planned. Since the entire production was to be purchased by the large manufacturer from outside the State, apart from any sales that might happen to be made to public sector organizations, there was no marketing department and no sales people were appointed.

Although the factory was designed to produce 4,000 fans per month, production started at a level of 30 fans per month and never exceeded a rate of 1,000. This was partly because of difficulties in the supply of components, such as die castings, and partly because the staff were not properly trained, the management was not effective and the machinery was not correctly planned. The pricing of the fans sold to the large manufacturer led to continuous disputes. The manufacturer was forced, because of the competitive nature of the industry, to give very generous discounts to its own dealers, and they claimed that the SIDECO unit should sell fans to them at a 14% discount from the net price at which they sold the fans to their dealers. They claimed that they could not otherwise afford to compete with other manufacturers, and the fans would therefore be unsaleable. The agreement was in fact ambiguous, in that it referred to a 14% discount from the 'effective selling price of the manufacturer to its dealers': SIDECO argued that this referred to the normal selling prices, while the manufacturer claimed that it referred to their net selling prices after giving away the discount. As a result of the disagreement the manufacturers refused to purchase the fans and nine months worth of production lay unsold in the factory. SIDECO were not allowed, under the agreement, to sell the fans direct to the public.

A number of the fans rusted while in storage for so long, and over 5,000 of them had to be unpacked, cleaned and reworked and then repacked ready for sale. As a result of this and the low production the factory lost money. During the year ending in March 1982 the loss totalled some $90,000. SIDECO asked the auditors to examine the situation; they concluded that the factory would only break even at a production rate of 2,500 fans per month and that 42 additional workers would have to be recruited in order to achieve this level. In addition, a further $150,000 would have to be invested in the enterprise. The SIDECO management knew that they were now free not to renew the agreement with their collaborator, but they realized that this alone would not solve all the problems of the business.

Comment

Government may have a role to play in assisting and encouraging small enterprises, but Government is unlikely to be able to make a success of running such enterprises itself. A small-scale unit, such as the SIDECO fan factory, does not automatically share the advantages of small scale simply because it is not a large production unit. Flexibility, rapid response and committed management are a function of individual ownership rather than any particular scale of unit.

The initial contract seems to have been remarkably loose, and generally favourable to the large manufacturer. It is unlikely that a private investor would have entered into an agreement of this sort, and the Corporation might have been better advised at the outset to encourage a private investor to enter fan manufacturing, possibly on a joint venture basis, and the private investor himself would undoubtedly have ensured that the agreement was not one-sided. Given the existing situation, however, SIDECO might consider making a clearer agreement with another fan manufacturer, or might try to carry on the operation on its own, without the collaboration of the large manufacturer, so that SIDECO could sell fans to the general public in Kerela and beyond.

The inevitable disadvantages of public ownership would still apply, however, and it would probably be better for SIDECO to attempt to identify a private investor who could take over the business and make a success of it on an independent basis. The assets could be purchased from SIDECO for cash, or over time on the basis of performance, and SIDECO could provide assistance in terms of introduction to any joint venture partners, guarantees of compliance with agreements, preferred access to public sector markets or other facilities. Their objective should be to create a genuinely viable fan manufacturing industry in the State and this is unlikely to be attained by a prolongation of public ownership.

SOLOMON PINO,
PANAMA

Solomon Pino had run his small clothing factory profitably for seven years in the capital city of Panama. He was no accountant, however; he did not even know what 'working capital' meant.

Solomon's friend Pedro Gonzalez, a shoe maker, had learnt something about book-keeping and accounts at a course given by the Small Business Department of the Ministry of Commerce and Industry in Panama. He talked to Solomon about what he learnt and although his shoe shop never seemed to be short of anything he needed, he always complained that he was short of working capital; Solomon Pino could not understand what his friend Pedro was complaining about.

Solomon was nevertheless concerned that he was ignorant about something which was felt to be necessary for small business success, so he went to the Small Business Department himself to ask their advice. The Officer whom he saw asked for a balance sheet and sent an Extension Officer to visit Solomon's factory and check if all was well.

Solomon had his accounts prepared every year by a professional Accountant in order to satisfy the legal requirements, and he was quite satisifed with the service he received. He realized however, that he had no qualified book-keeper of his own and he did not really know how to use his figures at all. He showed the following balance sheet, which described the position at the end of March 1980, to the adviser from the Small Business Department.

Solomon thought that this was easy enough to follow; all his customers paid cash except for one shop which had bought from him for many years. The stock of raw materials was all in his factory and was easy to check, including cloth, zippers, patterns, thread, hangers, labels and so on. There were not very many current assets but he seemed to have no trouble running the business.

As for the liabilities, Solomon had a $5,000 line of credit from the bank and therefore his present debt of $3,000 did not seem to present any problem. The accounts payable figure of $5,000 looked a little high and Solomon decided to analyze it more carefully. He knew that his sales were around $150,000 for a year, or an average of $12,500 a month. He also knew that the cost of raw materials and supplies normally amounted to about 10% of sales; in order to sell $12,500 worth of goods in a month he would have to buy approximately $1,250 worth of raw material. The $5,000 figure for accounts payable on the balance sheet would therefore be the equivalent of four months' purchases. Solomon knew that his suppliers only gave him 30 days' credit, so this meant he must be well behind on some of his bills; he wondered whether the figure of $5,000 meant that he was falling behind, that he had been buying particularly heavily recently or that there were some accounts payable which were not for raw materials.

Solomon Pino
Balance Sheet as at 31 March, 1980

Current Assets	$	Current Liabilities	$
Cash	1,100	Accounts Payable	5,000
Accounts Receivable	500	Short Term Bank Loan	3,000
Raw Materials	800	Mortgage Payments	
		Currently Due	3,000
	2,400		11,000
Fixed Assets		Long Term Liabilities	
Machinery and		Bank Loan	3,000
Equipment Net of		Retained Earnings	2,000
Depreciation	14,600	Original Investment	1,000
Total Assets	$17,000	Total Liabilities	$17,000

He discussed the problem with the adviser from the Small Business Department and soon found the answer. His sales had been around the normal level for February and March, but on analysing his list of accounts payable he found that all the individual items were for raw materials, except for one bill for $3,800 for advertisements. He therefore owed only $1,200 for raw materials out of the total and this was in line with the 30 day payment terms that he received.

The only other item of current liabilities was the amount due on the mortgage and as this was a routine payment on the ten year loan which he had received from the National Financial Corporation for his equipment, which had originally totalled $30,000, the figure seemed reasonable enough.

Pedro Gonzalez, however, had told Solomon that 'working capital' was the difference between his current assets and current liabilities, and that he himself liked to keep his current assets at twice the level of his current liabilities. He admitted that he was not always able to do this.

Solomon compared Pedro's situation with his own; the adviser from the Small Business Department had helped Solomon to analyze his own current assets and liabilities and although each item seemed reasonable enough, the total of current liabilities, at $11,000, was almost eleven times the current assets. Solomon realized that far from achieving Pedro's goal of current assets being double the level of current liabilities, he himself was actually in quite the reverse position.

In spite of this, however, Solomon did not have any problem with his business. He wondered whether every business was in fact different; perhaps his own working capital situation was in fact perfectly satisfactory for the type of business he had. In his business, where nearly all his sales were made for cash but his suppliers were willing to extend him credit for his purchases, might it not be perfectly acceptable for the current liabilities to exceed current assets by such a wide margin?

He concluded that his position as shown on his balance sheet was perfectly satisfactory for his business in its present condition. He had enough cash to pay his debts as they fell due and was always able to buy raw materials to keep the business operating properly. He discussed his conclusions with Pedro Gonzalez and decided that there would be no purpose in his going to attend one of the courses as Pedro had suggested. The rules which Pedro had learnt did not seem to apply to his business and he wondered whether there was any purpose in keeping accounts at all.

Comment

This case study illustrates the somewhat unorthodox, but often perfectly satisfactory, way in which some small businesses operate. It also shows how courses in book-keeping, if they are not taught properly, can actually lead to small business people's rejection of any form of record keeping, whereas they may actually need some records and could gain a great deal from them.

So far as can be seen, Solomon Pino is receiving the vast bulk of his sales in cash, from day to day, while the bills for his materials, and presumably for his wages and so on as well, fall due at the end of the month so that he has a 'float' which builds up during the month and is then exhausted by the payments which are made at the end.

His ratio of current liabilities to current assets may be totally out of line with what is normally expected, but since he is in the rather unusual situation of selling nearly everything for cash but being able to delay his payments until the end of each month, this is not in itself a problem. His business is also very highly geared, that is his own capital only makes up a very small proportion of the total investment. This is often inevitable when people of humble means start a business, and there is no reason why banks or other institutions should not be willing to extend credit as they have to Solomon Pino, particularly if they are able to use the assets such as machinery as security for their loan.

Solomon's friend Pedro is clearly confused by the typically standardized and rigid set of rules which he has apparently learnt in his book-keeping course. Every small business is different, not only in terms of the nature of the business but of the ability of its owner. Some people may be able to keep quite sophisticated accounts, and, what is more important, to make good use of them; others may only be able to operate the most rudimentary systems or may indeed be totally illiterate. This feature of small enterprises, which is not shared by large businesses which can afford to employ trained accountants, only strengthens the case for individual advisory services such as Solomon has received, as a complement to or even a substitute for classroom courses. An individual adviser can appreciate the situation of each business and, if he has been properly trained, can recommend and help to install a system which is appropriate for the business and its owner. In the classroom such individual treatment is generally impossible.

The result of Solomon's discussions with his friend, or indeed the likely result if he himself went to a course, has been to make him altogether disillusioned with book-keeping. He could, however, make very good use of a simple cash flow planning system in order to ensure that he is able to pay his various large bills such as mortgage repayments and advertising accounts when they fall due, and that he is able to invest any surplus cash he may have in a savings account in order to earn some interest in the meantime. A well-trained adviser should be able to show him how he can use a simple set of records in this way, and thus motivate him to learn how to keep them. Figures such as he has at the moment may be useful for the taxation department, and perhaps for analysts who are deciding whether or not to lend the business money, but because the owner of the business himself has no idea what they mean he is unlikely to make the Accountant's task easier by keeping the proper original documents, and is not getting full value for the money he spends on having the figures prepared.

THE STAREHE GENERAL ENGINEERING SOCIETY, KENYA

The Starehe Boys Centre is a vocational school in a poor area of Nairobi in Kenya. It is run by a voluntary organization, and aims to provide a general secondary education for boys from poor families who might otherwise be destitute. Most importantly, the Centre aims to equip its boys for a productive career by giving them an appropriate vocational training.

There are numerous other training institutions in Kenya, and in the mid 1970s a number of the boys who had been trained at the School started to find difficulty in obtaing employment, in spite of the quality of their training. One of the teachers in the Technical Training Department of the Centre, a Mr. D.J. Parry, decided that it would be a good idea to start a manufacturing company which would offer employment to some of the boys and would also earn profits to help in the funding of the Centre. He had earlier been associated with similar enterprises in Europe, and he wanted to use his experience for the benefit both of the School and the boys who had been trained there.

Mr. Parry prepared a proposal and submitted it to the Management Committee of the Starehe Boys Centre. They approved of the idea and they invited applicants from the boys who were leaving the School in 1978. There were a large number of applicants, and the Management Committee finally selected six boys who were leaving the School after six years of training, and a further six who were leaving after only four years. The enterprise was registered as the Starehe General Engineering Society in September 1978, with twelve members, and its stated objectives were to provide its members with employment, to provide financial aid to the Centre and to manufacture and sell general engineering products.

The members each contributed $30 towards the initial capital, and the Centre granted them a small piece of land within its compound so that they could construct a workshop and an accommodation block. It was intended that they would eventually be able to build a proper factory in the industrial area of the city. The Centre also offered to continue to accommodate the boys until their own accommodation block was completed, and in return for this and the right to use the land the Society undertook to donate its buildings to the Centre when they were finally able to move to proper industrial premises.

The members held their first meeting; after long debate and discussion they decided that they would manufacture simple equipment for local industry. They agreed that the six older boys would form the Management Committee and the younger ones would be the manufacturing team. Mr. Parry, the initiator of the Society, was to be its Secretary and designer.

The members realized that they had very little money to spend. They had had some training in building, and they set about the construction of their own workshop with great enthusiasm. They succeeded in raising a certain amount of extra capital from one or two private companies which took an interest in the Starehe Boys Centre, and they commissioned a private contractor to complete the building and to install the electrical connections. They started operations in January 1979, working initially in the Centre's workshops when they were not being used by the students. Work did not proceed very smoothly, because the facilities were not always available to them, but the members nevertheless maintained their enthusiasm and attracted some interest from other voluntary agencies in the area.

As a result of one of these contacts, they received a grant of $1,500 from a charitable organization based in Denmark; they decided to spend this money on specialized welding training for some of the members. During the second half of 1979 they started to receive more orders, mainly from the Starehe Centre itself and from international donor agencies who needed various items of equipment. In October of that year the Society received a major boost in the form of a grant of $30,000 from the European Economic Community, through the Save the Children Fund. This money was used to purchase machinery and to complete the workshop and an accommodation block for six of the members. The Society was now able to operate independently of the Centre and the members had great hopes for the future.

In spite of their new facilities, it proved very difficult to obtain orders. The Society only had enough work to employ about half the members, and most of the older boys, who had made up the Management Committee, left the Society at this stage because they were earning no money and their education meant that they could obtain jobs elsewhere. This actually proved to be for the benefit of the Society, since most of these boys had been in the Management Committee and had added to the overheads expenses without actually carrying out productive work. Some of them, however, had been involved in production, and this meant that some of the few orders which the Society had obtained were not delivered on time. Some new members were recruited from those who left the School in 1979, and they helped to complete the work but they were not as experienced as those who had left. During 1980 the Society succeeded in obtaining more orders and a further group of members were sent for advanced training in welding. There was still a shortage of working capital, however, and orders could only be accepted if customers were willing to make a 60% deposit in order to cover the costs of raw material. The Society's suppliers generously allowed them to buy raw material on credit, but the lack of finance made it impossible for them to manufacture prototypes in order to show their customers what they could do. During 1980 and 1981 the Society diversified its production into items such as coathangers, steel gates, wheelbarrows, fences and agricultural implements such as ploughs, hand-carts and threshing machines. They also produced some special items for particular contracts, such as a trailer for an international agricultural assistance agency, and a large number of steel lockers for the Ministry of Education and for the Starehe Boys Centre itself.

1982 proved to be the Society's best year. There was a steady flow of orders and all the members were reasonably well occupied. Towards the end of the year, however, the worsening economic situation reduced the level of orders. Raw materials went up in price and not all the increase could be passed on to customers. Because of the credit squeeze, the Society's suppliers were no longer able to allow them credit, and customers were also no longer willing to put down the 60% deposit which the Society required. Because of their financial problems the Society applied to the Co-operative Bank for a loan of $1,000 in order to build up their working capital, but their application was rejected because, so the Bank said, there was no money available.

At the end of 1983 Mr. Parry reviewed the past five years of operation and concluded that the Society had not achieved the majority of its objectives. They had failed to break into the market for specialized industrial equipment, as had been planned, and had instead been forced to manufacture whatever their customers asked just in order to survive. As a result, they had not developed any particular expertise and had had to accept work at very low margins of profit. Their operation was not really any different from the large number of informal mechanical workshops throughout the city of Nairobi, and as a result there was stiff competition and they could make very little surplus.

Because members had not been able to earn a reasonable wage from the Society, there had been a rapid turnover among them and hardly any of those who had originally joined in 1978 were still active members in 1983. The Society had paid for a number of its members to receive advanced welding training, but only one of these remained with the Society and the value of this investment was therefore lost as far as the other members were concerned. They hoped that two other members who had completed their Ordinary Diplomas at the Kenya Polytechnic, as a result of the training and experience they had acquired in the Co-operative, would remain with the Society but there was no guarantee that they would. Finally, the Society had on balance made a loss during the five years and had thus been unable to make any contributions to the Starehe Boys Centre as had originally been intended.

Mr. Parry had borne the main burden of managing the Society during the five years of its existence. In addition to his full-time job as a teacher at the School, he was effectively responsible for the sales, designing, estimating, ordering and accounts of the Co-operative. It was suggested that they needed to employ a Workshop Supervisor and a Salesman in order to reduce Mr. Parry's workload, but there was no way in which the Society could afford to pay these people from its own revenue. They applied to the Ministry of Co-operative Development, and to a number of voluntary organizations for technical assistance or volunteers, but without success.

Mr. Parry had still not lost sight of the Society's original intention to move from its temporary premises in the Starehe Boys Centre compound into the industrial area. He applied to Kenya Industrial Estates, a parastatal body which is responsible for financing and promoting small industries, and they tentatively agreed to finance the Society's expansion into one of their industrial areas. Mr. Parry, the members and the staff of the Centre sincerely hoped that this assistance would materialize.

Comment

It is perhaps unreasonable to expect young people to start a co-operative enterprise, or any other form of business, immediately they leave school, but it is also unlikely that any co-operative enterprise which is wholly initiated and effectively managed by outsiders will succeed for very long. In contrast to the more successful co-operative societies described in this book, the Starehe General Engineering Society was 'put together' by a foreigner, and the members themselves were selected by outsiders rather than coming together as the result of shared interests or adversity.

During the four years of its life which are described, the Society was almost continuously dependent on grants from voluntary organizations and on contracts from international agencies and others which would be unlikely to be given on a purely commercial basis. In addition, the most important single resource, namely management, was not provided by members themselves but was given on a part-time basis by the initiator of the enterprise. The Society was thus a 'sheltered' business, which did not have to stand up to the full force of competition, and this was somewhat paradoxical since the members were actually people who had received an above average level of training and might therefore have been expected to support themselves in a completely competitive environment. It would be impossible to put a value on all the grants, concessions, voluntary time and other resources which have been lavished on the group, but it may well be that the total cost of maintaining up to twelve people in employment would turn out to have been very high indeed. This may be necessary for handicapped people or others who are particularly disadvantaged, but it is probable that most if not all of the Society's members could have obtained other jobs for themselves if the Society had not existed.

It would certainly be in the interest of the Society and the Centre if it could move away to an industrial area and be exposed to the real world. It is unlikely, however, that the Society could survive very long in the formal environment of an industrial estate, and a less formal 'squatter type' location, perhaps similar to that which they are presently occupying but not close to the Centre, might be more appropriate for their stage of development. Such a location might be provided free of charge by one of the companies which supports the Centre, and the members would then be forced to manage their own business and depend on their own resources. It may be that they would fail, and this would obviously be a disappointment for Mr. Parry and for the Starehe Boys Centre as a whole. There must come a point, however, when any enterprise, particularly one involving people with better than average skills, must be cut loose from its origins and forced to face the real world. If it fails, its members will have gained some valuable experience and will probably be able to obtain employment elsewhere. It is probable, however, that at least some part of the Society will survive, perhaps on a far more modest basis, or reconstituted as a private business, and other people will undoubtedly make good use of the buildings and equipment if they are allowed to do so. The sponsors may lose some 'face', but the physical assets and experience that have been accumulated will not be wasted.

THE STATE POTTERY VENTURE, INDIA

The States of India vary very much in their wealth and industrialization. Some are heavily industrialized, while the people of others depend almost entirely on agriculture, apart from a few small-scale industries and traditional handicrafts. The Governments of those States that are particularly backward are attempting to promote industry in every way, and in 1970 the Government of one of the States decided to set up joint ventures between its own State Small Industries Coporation and local investors. They hoped that they would in this way be able to demonstrate the viability of non-traditional industries in the State, and also to tap the substantial savings of the wealthier farmers, by persuading them to invest in the new ventures.

The State Small Industries Corporation is wholly owned by the State Government and it was decided that they would hold 51% of the equity of the new ventures, while 49% would be held by one or more local investors. The intention was that the enterprises would be expected to break even within four or five years and that the private investors would then buy the Corporation's shares at a fair value to be assessed by independent auditors. If they did not wish to buy the Corporation's shares then they could be offered to anybody else who was interested.

In pursuance of this policy a pottery company was incorporated in June 1972. The plan was to produce some 900 tons of crockery every year, and the total capital investment was about $200,000. The Corporation invested $110,000, partly as a loan and partly as equity, local investors provided $70,000 and the balance was provided by the normal Government capital subsidy of 15% of the fixed assets.

Three and a half years went by before production started. During this time the cost of the equipment, and the sums necessary for working capital, rose substantially. The delay was unavoidable, because of the legal procedures which were demanded by the financing institutions before they could disburse their funds. Some of the private investors' contribution was to be made in kind, in land and buildings, and the Corporation demanded that these assets, along with the investors' money, should be formally committed to the enterprise before they themselves would disburse any money. At the same time, they demanded that the private investors should accept the Corporation's valuation of their contribution, without any recourse to arbitration.

At a fairly early point in the discussions on this and other issues, the Corporation deemed that their funds had indeed been committed to the new venture, although it had not yet started operation. As a result, interest started to be levied on the loan portion of the finance, and the total amount of interest which had accrued was deducted from the actual amount which was disbursed when the assets were actually purchased. As a result, fewer funds than had originally had been agreed were available, and although the private investors still owned 49% of the equity, their actual share of the investment was larger than had been agreed.

After all these problems had been resolved, the necessary equipment was bought and installed and production finally started early in 1976. The management had carried out a detailed market survey in order to identify the best markets for their products, and they had found that the most promising market was the numerous roadside restaurants throughout the State. The Company appointed dealers who had access to the owners of these restaurants, and substantial initial orders were placed. In spite of this success, however, a number of problems prevented the Company from taking advantage of the demand for its products They found it difficult to purchase enough coal to operate their kilns, the electricity was unreliable and they could not always buy diesel fuel for their standby generator or for transport. It was difficult to recruit good staff and skilled labour, and neither the State nor the central Government gave them any marketing support. There is in India a scheme whereby small-scale enterprises are given a 15% price preference when bidding for Government contracts. Joint ventures such as the State Potteries Company, however, are not regarded as small-scale units for the purposes of this scheme, since the State Government holds a majority of their equity. They have therefore to sell through intermediaries and thus to incur additional marketing expenditure.

By the end of 1982 the Company had almost ceased operation. The highest production ever achieved, which was in the first year of operations, was 186 tons, but by 1982 this had fallen to twelve tons. The Company had accumulated losses of over $150,000, and it owed a total of $300,000 to the State Small Industries Corporation, various banks and to its employees. This was in addition to the $70,000 which had been invested by private people in the State.

The State Small Industries Corporation called in a number of consultants to investigate the affairs of the Company; they concluded that its major problem by this time was a shortage of working capital. They recommended that the Company's debts should be cancelled and that the Corporation and the private investors should contribute additional funds. The private investors refused to contribute any more money to the Company, and the State Small Industries Corporation is prohibited by the Company's Articles of Association from contributing more than 51% of its equity. The only way to obtain additional funds was for the Corporation to extend a short term unsecured loan and they accordingly did this. By this time, however, the private investors were due to take over the ownership of the whole Company. They were naturally unwilling to do this, even if they could obtain the Corporation's shares for nothing, because they would be taking on the Company's liabilities for repayment of its loans.

The Corporation decided to try to sell the Company to anyone who was willing to take it on, but nobody replied to their advertisement. Together with the State Bank, they had the right to dispose of the Company in any way they wished, but it appeared to be impossible to do this and at the same time to maintain the private investors' interest which had been one of the main objectives of the scheme. The Company could only be viable, they thought, if additional funds were invested and this could only be done if it was liquidated and reconstituted as a Government–owned enterprise.

One possibility was for the State Small Industries Corporation to liquidate the Company, pay off the debts and use the building and equipment as a common facility centre in order to assist small-scale potters in the area and to enable them to become self–employed. Alternatively, the assets might be sold to any private entrepreneur who was willing to take them on, without the accompanying liabilities, or the Corporation itself might take over and manage the enterprise. Since the main activity of the Corporation was to distribute iron and steel raw materials to small industries, its management were not enthusiastic about becoming involved in the long-term ownership and management of a quite unrelated enterprise. Nevertheless, some way had to be found of achieving the original objectives of diversifying industries within the State and creating employment for local people.

Comment

It might quite reasonably be argued that the State should not become involved in the actual ownership and management of small enterprises in a country where the private ownership of buisness is generally encouraged. According to this argument, private entrepreneurs will on their own take advantage of any opportunities that become available, and if they do not this only means that for some reason or another the enterprise is not economic. It is even less likely to be economic if it is managed by Government staff.

It is more generally accepted, however, that Government does have a role to play in initiating new activities, and in demonstrating that they are viable. The basic premise behind the scheme under which the Pottery Company was set up was that Government's involvement should be strictly temporary. Private entrepreneurs were for one reason or another unaware of the opportunities that existed. Government had a responsibility to take the initial risk and to lead the way for numerous other private investors in the future.

Clearly in such circumstances there will inevitably be a risk, and it is likely to be rather larger than that which private entrepreneurs would be willing to take, since otherwise they would have taken it. In these circumstances, Government is hardly to be blamed if they turn out to have made a mistake, and the venture turns out not to be viable. The problem is that Government officials are reluctant to admit their mistakes, and are likely to continue 'pouring good money after bad' in a way that no private businessman could. They stand to lose prestige and status if something that they have proposed turns out to have been a mistake, but the money that has to be spent to keep it going does not come out of their pockets.

The initial scheme may have been basically a reasonable one, although some provisions of the agreement between the private investors and the Government might reasonably have been changed. The basic problem seems, however, to have been that private business people were in fact correct when they decided not to invest in pottery industries in the State. The local market was insufficient, and supplies of power, fuel and so on were inadequate for a viable enterprise. If the business could only have survived on the basis of the preferential scheme for Government contracts, this would not have been evidence of its genuine profitability.

It may be, however, that a private investor would be willing to take the risk of continuing the enterprise, particularly if he could acquire the necessary plant and equipment at a substantial discount from its real cost. People might suggest that it would be 'unfair' to allow a private individual to take over the assets of the Company at a low price, but if a genuine free auction can be arranged this would in fact reflect their true value. The major investment is presumably in kilns, which cannot easily be moved, so the facilities are likely to be used for making pottery, in their present location, if they can be used at all. The State Small Industries Corporation should therefore liquidate the Company and sell the assets for whatever they can fetch. The Corporation and the bankers may have to write off some proportion of their loans, but the mistake was made when the enterprise was originally set up. Their objective now should be to maximize the chances of the equipment being used to achieve the original objectives of the scheme.

TDL TAILORS, KENYA

Two businessmen who had had some experience in the clothing trade decided to start their own tailoring business in Nairobi in Kenya. They formed a partnership in 1978 and registered the business under the name of TDL Tailors.

They drew up a scheme for presentation to the bank, suggesting a total investment of $46,000 which was to cover machinery and equipment, together with an allowance for working capital. They planned to implement the enterprise in two stages, the second following the first after six months or so, and this sum of money was sufficient for the complete venture.

They presented the proposal to the local development bank, which was empowered to lend money for both fixed and working capital. The bank's staff decided that it would be unwise to advance the total amount in the first instance; they argued that the enterprise should prove itself in its first phase, and should then present a further application for funding for the second stage if the results were by then satisfactory. They believed this to be advisable because it would take time for the partners to find a market for the products of their business, and tailoring business is in any case very seasonal since it depends on school uniform contracts and other official work which is not offered throughout the year.

The total cost of the first phase was $30,000; after some discussion the bank agreed to lend the partners 70% of this amount, or $21,000, to cover the machinery and equipment and its instalation. The partners were themselves supposed to contribute the balance of $9,000 to finance the working capital requirements of the business.

Once they had obtained the money, however, the partners did not act as the bank had recommended. They only contributed $5,000 themselves, rather than the $9,000 which they had agreed, and they spent virtually the whole of the money they had obtained from the bank, and their own contribution, on machinery and equipment, leaving very little for working capital. They also bought a car, arguing that it would be useful for the business but knowing very well that they would also find it very convenient to use for their own purposes.

The bank was quite unaware of what the partners had done, because they did not have enough staff to follow up investments of this sort, and since there was a two year grace period before any

Profit and Loss Account for TDL Tailors
for Year Ended 31 December 1979

	$	$
Sales		40,000
Materials		
Opening Stock	6,600	
Purchases	23,000	
	29,600	
Less: Closing Stock	6,200	
Cost of Materials		23,400
Gross Margin		17,200
Expenses		
Wages and Salaries	4,200	
Transport	2,800	
Rent	1,000	
Maintenance and Depreciation	1,600	
Other Miscellaneous Expenses	3,300	
Bank Interest	800	
Bad Debts	1,000	
		14,700
Net Profit		$ 2,500

Balance Sheet for TDL Tailors as at 31 December 1979

Current Assets	$	Liabilities	$
Cash and Bank Balance	500	Accounts Payable	3,500
Accounts Receivable	1,000	Bank Overdraft	4,600
Stocks	6,200	Long Term Bank Loan	20,000
		Re-invested Profits	1,500
Fixed Assets		Original Investment	5,000
Vehicle	2,000		
Machinery and			
Equipment	24,900		
Total Assets	$34,600	Total Liabilities	$34,600

repayments were due there was no way in which the bank could discover what was actually happening.

The partners intended to sell most of their products to Government and schools, since they had good connections with people who gave contracts for school and office uniforms. Contract supplies of this sort are meant to be paid for in cash on delivery of the goods, but because individual Government Departments and schools have to submit all bills for approval to their headquarters substantial delays usually occur. There was not enough money to enable the partners to buy more raw material, and to pay their workers, while they were waiting for Government Departments to pay for goods they had already received, and as a result the business was unable to operate at more than a quarter of its full capacity. As the bank had warned, the contracts were also not available all the year and this made their problems even worse.

As a result, the business lost $800 in its first year and only made a profit of $2,300 in the second year, which was about a quarter of what they had expected. There was insufficient cash to repay the first instalment of the bank loan when it fell due and when the partners requested further finance from the bank they met with a refusal; the bank's staff argued that their performance during the first phase confirmed that it had been right not to finance the whole enterprise at once, since they had not shown themselves capable of managing the business and its finances properly.

Comment

Development banks often restrict themselves to the provision of capital for the purchase of fixed assets, leaving working capital to be provided by a traditional commercial bank. Entrepreneurs who have not had the time to develop commercial banking relationships are thus deprived of working capital, and many new enterprises fail for this reason.

This does not appear to have happened in this case, since the development bank was far-sighted enough to provide working capital as well as fixed capital, and the partners appeared to have obtained an overdraft from a commercial bank as well.

They appear, however, not to have understood the need for money to finance their day to day operations as well as for the purchase of the machinery. Many financial institutions attempt to avoid this type of problem by supervising borrowers regularly, or by controlling the use of money by paying for equipment direct to suppliers and not giving cash to borrowers at all. This type of measure involves a substantial administrative burden, however, and it may be that this development bank was unable to undertake this.

From the figures it appears that the interest rate was only 4%; if this is the case, it is hardly surprising that the development bank was unable to afford sufficient supervision, since the transaction probably involved a loss even before any administrative expenses had been taken into account. The interest rate could well have been doubled, or increased even more, without having too serious an effect on the economics of the enterprise; It would at the same time enormously improve the economics of the deal from the bank's point of view, and thus allow them to carry out the necessary supervizion.

In addition, the bank does not seem to have ensured that the investors committed their own funds, as agreed, before disbursing its own money. Measures of this sort not only protect the lender's interest, but also, in the long term, protects the interests of the borrowers themselves.

The investors believe, as is so often the case, that their problems can be solved by more capital. The figures, however, show that their problem arises not so much from large sums of money owing to them by customers, as from the large amount of unsold stocks they have accumulated. If the bankers analyse the figures correctly, they will be unlikely to extend further finance until and unless the partners drastically reduce the stocks, if necessary by reducing their prices, and they should possibly be advised to sell the vehicle as well. It may be that through these measures they can secure the necessary working capital to revive the enterprise without any further money from the bank. It is arguable that the bank should have insisted that the investors displayed some knowledge of financial management before extending the loan to them. The present situation will test their ability to manage an enterprise of this kind; if they succeed in redeploying the assets effectively they will indicate that they can make good use of further resources, but may not even have need of them; if they do not succeed, they will demonstrate that they are not fit to run the business and the bank would probably be doing the right thing to demand repayment and if necessary foreclose so that the productive assets could be transferred to other investors who were better able to make use of them.

USHIRIKA WA KIKOSI CHA UGENZI – THE BUILDING BRIGADE CO-OPERATIVE, TANZANIA

Tanga is the second largest city of Tanzania, with a population of well over 100,000 people. Towards the end of 1973 there was a serious fire in the city, which destroyed a number of buildings. There were not enough building contractors in the town to undertake all the construction work that was necessary, and a number of politicians and members of the local and central Governments decided to use the opportunity in order to promote a builders' co-operative society.

The co-operative movement plays a very fundamental part in the political and economic life of Tanzania, and politicians in particular are always ready to grasp any opportunity to promote co-operative enterprises.

They succeeded in identifying 38 stone masons and carpenters who used to work individually, or on a casual basis for other contractors. They were willing to be organized into a co-operative, since they thought that this might be a way in which they could earn rather more money from the rebuilding programme than if they were working for other people. The politicians also encouraged them to join by pointing out that the society would be in a better position to offer them continuing employment after the rebuilding programme was completed, and as members they could take advantage of the numerous Government programmes which have been set up to assist co-operative societies.

Each of the members contributed $10 for the share capital and they selected a Chairman, a Secretary and a Treasurer. They appointed a Committee of ten other members who were to be responsible for the day to day running of their Society, and it was formally registered as a co-operative on 20 February 1974.

The Government provided building materials free of charge to the Society for use in the reconstruction programme, since they had a responsibility to help people who had suffered in the fire. The owners of the buildings paid similar prices to what they would have paid to independent contractors, less the cost of materials, and the members received wages similar to what they were used to being paid by their previous employers. There was a substantial surplus and this was distributed to members according to their level of skill. It was difficult to determine exactly how each member had contributed to the work, and how skilled he was, and a number of the members were therefore very discontented at the way the surplus was distributed. No up to date records were kept of the money that had been received, or the way it had been distributed, but the members had made more money than they would have done otherwise and were therefore willing to remain with the Society.

After the initial reconstruction programme had been completed, there was no other obvious work for the Society. The Government then decided to make them a loan of $1,500 in order to enable them to establish a carpentry shop and to bid for Government tenders for school desks and office furniture. The Society bid for a number of tenders and were awarded a fair proportion of them, both because they were a co-operative society and because their prices were very reasonable. They had little or no machinery and they therefore borrowed $12,500 from the Small Industries Development Organization to purchase equipment. They also had little or no working capital, since nearly all the surplus from their original work had been distributed; they successfully negotiated overdraft facilities with the National Bank of Commerce for an initial sum of $2,500 which was later increased to $10,000.

The Society successfully completed all the orders they had received. A number of the contracts were finished somewhat later than had been promised, but because their customers were quite satisfied with the quality of the work all the bills were paid in full. The delays arose because of production inefficiencies which increased overheads – jobs were taking longer to complete than had been expected. Further problems arose because some of the Committee Members were suspected of misappropriating funds but nothing could be proved because there were no proper records. At the end of their first year the Society failed to produce any proper accounts and this severely eroded members' faith in the Society.

At this point a number of the members, including some of the officials, decided to leave and to start working on their own once more. It was impossible to identify the people who had misappropriated the funds of the Society, or to calculate how much had been stolen, but there was certainly not enough money to start repaying the various loans which the Society had obtained. The National Bank of Commerce threatened to seize the equipment which had been pledged to them as security for the overdraft, but they discovered that the same equipment had already been pledged to the Small Industries Development Organization as security for the long term loan.

After one or two more years membership had fallen to about 20 members, but they actually spent most of their time working for themselves. The Society totally lost its reputation for quality work, which it had gained at the beginning, and it ceased to receive any further contracts. None of the officials provided any consistent leadership, and nobody took the trouble to submit bids on the Society's behalf. One or two of the members occasionally made pieces of furniture on a speculative basis in the Society's premises, when they had no other private work, but apart from this the Society was virtually moribund.

The accounts showed total debts of $32,800, including those owed to the Small Industries Development Organization and the National Bank of Commerce, and there appeared to be little chance of either institution recovering its money. Because the Society had not kept proper records, nor allowed for depreciation, and the equipment had in any case not been well maintained, it was doubtful whether it could be sold for the figures at which it was valued in the accounts. In addition, the dispute between the two institutions over the security meant that neither could foreclose; the commercial bank also said that they had a claim on the stock of the Society, but this was valueless since there were no stocks of raw materials or finished goods.

The Building Brigade Co-operative
Balance Sheet as at 30 September, 1980

Liabilities	$	Assets	$
Members Share Capital	380	Land and Buildings	6,200
Small Industries Development		Tools and Equipment	24,980
Organization, Long Term		Office Furniture	1,700
Loan	12,500	Accounts Receivable	300
Bank Overdraft	12,000	Cash	nil
Accounts Payable	8,300		
Total Liabilities	$ 33,180	Total Assets	$ 33,180

Comment

This Co-operative Society was started by politicians as an ideological gesture, and in no way arose from the initiative or the genuine needs of its members. They would in any case have obtained employment in the reconstruction after the fire, and they were only willing to join because they saw that the Society might marginally improve their livelihood.

After the Society was started and obtained its first contract its intiators appeared to have lost interest in it. Nobody else, including the members, was unduly concerned with the survival of the Society and nobody seems to have cared very much when it virtually ceased to exist. This is hardly surprising, since it was not started in response to any serious felt need in the members, and it then failed significantly to improve their incomes thereafter.

The financing institutions seem, in their enthusiasm for the new co-operative, to have failed to protect their investment as they should. The claims to security are confused, and the value of the assets which are said to have been pledged as collateral has not been properly protected. Inefficiency of this kind is a dis-service to the owners of the financial institutions, who are in this case society as a whole, and it is also of no long-term advantage to the borrowers. If as a result of this type of negligence they fail to repay their loans, they will lose whatever credit rating they may have had and will be unable to obtain further funds in the future. Financial institutions have a duty to ensure the recovery of their funds and in so doing they can play a substantial role in improving the management of the enterprises which borrow from them.

Since the Building Brigade Co-operative has ceased to offer any useful services either to its members or its customers, there is no point in anyone attempting to prolong its existence. The financial institutions should recognize that the loans which they have made to the Society may have to be written down. Imported capital equipment is particularly scarce in Tanzania and the machinery now lying idle in the Society's workshop should be put to good use, in order to help in the generation of employment, by anybody who is able to demonstrate their capacity to employ it.

THE WAHIRA MECHANICAL WORKSHOP, NIGERIA

Saidu Tarfa was a Vehicle Inspection Officer with the Government of what used to be the north-eastern State of Nigeria. When Gongola State was created in February 1976 Tarfa decided to retire from the Government service and to establish a motor repair workshop with his retirement gratuity. He was a skilled mechanic, he had extensive contacts with all the major private companies and Government organizations who operated fleets of vehicles and he also had contacts with other people in Government who would help him in his enterprise.

Through his friends at the Ministry responsible for allocation of land he was able to obtain a plot in the local industrial estate and they also gave him useful advice on the construction of his workshop. He hired a number of skilled motor mechanics and successfully overcame the normal problems associated with the beginning of a business. He worked hard and supervized his mechanics closely, and as a result a number of individual civil servants and Government establishments became his major customers.

As his business expanded Tarfa realized that he needed more finance for new equipment and for working capital. He approached his friends in the Government and they directed him to the State Ministry of Trade, Industry and Co-operatives who were operating a small industries credit scheme. Tarfa made some inquiries about what was required, and submitted an application for a loan of $80,000.

The staff responsible for the credit scheme asked the Industrial Development Centre at Zaria to help them appraise the application. This was a Federal institution which was responsible for appraising the technical aspects of applications submitted to the State credit scheme. Officials from this Centre, together with staff from the State Ministry, visited Tarfa's workshop and interviewed him at some length. They prepared a detailed pre-investment proposal and finally recommended a loan of $60,000; Tarfa built a new workshop and equipped it with the most modern machinery.

Tarfa's business now became extremely successful. He bought a new Volvo car for his own use, built a small hotel and established the Wahira Driving School. Because of the good service available at his workshop people stopped taking their cars to the neighbouring States and gave him all their business. Tarfa was appointed as an agent for a vehicle insurance company and was thus empowered to inspect vehicles which had been involved in accidents and to recommend what compensation should be paid to their owners.

In September 1978 one of the driving school cars was involved in an accident and the student was killed. Tarfa was sued and paid a heavy fine and the driving school was closed down. This was the beginning of his downfall. The ban on political activities in the country had recently been lifted and Tarfa became Chairman of a political party in the State. He became so involved in politics that he paid little attention to his business and was no longer able to spend much time in his workshop supervising his mechanics. He employed a Manager to share responsibility with the Foreman but spare parts became increasingly difficult to obtain and the Manager and the Foreman both became more concerned to make money for themselves than to run the workshop properly. Most of Tarfa's customers deserted him, and his good mechanics also left as they saw their earnings drop.

At the same time two large vehicle distribution companies which had not previously operated in Gongola State opened well-stocked workshops in the town. Both these companies were very well organized and could provide efficient and rapid service at reasonable prices; the various Government Departments who had previously sent all their vehicles to Tarfa's workshop now directed that all their vehicles should be sent to one or other of the new companies. Tarfa had originally been regarded as one of the most reliable borrowers from the small industries credit scheme; he was now in arrears to the extent of almost $15,000, and there seemed little chance that he would ever catch up with his payments.

Comment

Tarfa was apparently well qualified for his enterprise. He had extremely appropriate Government experience and extensive contacts with people who could be helpful to him. On the face of it, therefore, the decision to lend money to him was correct. Events proved that it was a mistake; is there any way in which those responsible for approving the loan might have been expected to avoid their error?

The main determinant of the success of any new enterprise is the man or woman who starts it. In this case, however, most of the investigation appears to have been directed at the financial and the technical aspects of the venture, rather than at Tarfa himself. The technical appraisal was carried out by an institution whose staff were unlikely to have any personal knowledge of the entrepreneur, and detailed feasibility studies and pre-investment proposals are no substitute for careful inquiries and consideration of the personality of whoever is borrowing the money.

Success clearly went to Tarfa's head; he diversified into a number of different enterprises, thus increasing the complexity of his management task, and started to live extravagantly. Worst of all, he entered politics. There is, in most developing countries, a serious shortage of people with the necessary education, ability and ambition to go into politics, and very few of them are wealthy enough to be able to spend time in establishing a political position. As a result, many business people are diverted from their enterprises by the lure of politics, and political success is also expected to bring commercial rewards. This may be an unavoidable problem for countries which were prevented by colonial domination from developing indigenous political institutions. From the point of view of small business, bankers should probably avoid lending to people with political inclinations, and business people should avoid politics.

The staff of the credit scheme might or might not have been able to avoid making the mistake of lending Tarfa money in the first place; now that he is in arrears, he may use his political position to prevent them from securing the money from him. If possible, however, they should take all the necessary steps to recover their money; the assets which were purchased with the loan should have been pledged as security, and the staff of the scheme should be willing to go so far as to seize them and auction them off if the money is not forthcoming. If Tarfa knows that this is a real threat, he will probably sell the business or take other steps which will enable him to repay the loan and avoid the embarrassment of a public auction of his business.

STADI FURNITURE CO-OPERATIVE SOCIETY LIMITED, TANZANIA

There were a number of privately owned furniture manufacturers in and around Arusha in Tanzania. Because there was a surplus of skilled labour in the area, they were able to hire good carpenters for very low wages and a number of these companies exploited this situation; they paid little or no regard to the well being or commitment of their workers. In 1978 fifteen carpenters who worked in factories of this sort decided to leave their jobs and to start a co-operative society in order to improve their situation.

After some discussion five of the original people left, and on 18 October 1978 the ten remaining carpenters registered their society as the Stadi Furniture Co-operative Society Limited. They decided that each member had to pay a membership fee of $2 and must also purchase a minimum of seven shares for $10 each. They also determined that every member must be a carpenter and must work full time at the Society's workshop with the other members. A number of other people would have liked to join and to learn a trade with the Society but were prevented from joining by this particular regulation.

The Society eventually succeeded in renting premises for $22 a month; they later built a partition across this building and it has been their workshop ever since. At the beginning they found that their limited funds were insufficient to buy the equipment they needed. They approached the Small Industries Development Organisation early in 1979. At that time, by coincidence, the Organisation had on its hands a mechanical planer which they had imported for a private workshop owner who had then proved unable to pay for it. The machine was worth $6,800, and the local Director of the Small Industries Development Organisation was very happy to transfer this machine to the new Society, in the form of a loan. Later in the same year the Society purchased a band saw for $2,800 and a circular saw for $2,500 from the Organization on the same basis. With these three machines they were now as well equipped as most private workshops and only the final finishing jobs still had to be done by hand.

From the outset a number of the private furniture companies did their best to make life difficult for the new Society, partly because they resented the fact that their workers had set up in competition with their previous employers in this way, and partly because they naturally wished to resist any new competitive enterprise. The political climate in Tanzania favours co-operative enterprises, and as a result a number of large buyers in the region, such as the General Tyre Company, the Army and the local Department of the Ministry of Co-operative Development gave the new Society some trial business. They were agreeably surprised by the quality and price, and as a result continued to support the Co-operative with contracts for the manufacture of office furniture. Private people within these organizations observed the quality of the furniture which was being supplied by the Co-operative and started to place orders for individual pieces of furniture for their own use. The word soon spread, and other individual customers started to place orders with the Society.

Although none of the members of the Society had any training in management or administration, and only one had had any technical education beyond primary school, they all recognized the importance of using good raw materials, producing quality work and delivering goods on time. The main wood they use is camphor, which grows in the Kilimanjaro Region, near to Arusha, and they have enough experience to know whether the wood is dry enough to be used or not. They normally store all the timber they buy for at least a month in a dry place and this means that the furniture they make does not warp.

The Committee Members produce regular budgets and prepare work schedules on the basis of the orders they receive and the delivery times requested by their customers. They submit tenders for as many contracts as possible, and business of this sort plays an important part in their total turnover. The workload inevitably varies; rather than take on new full time members, who might not be able to be fully employed throughout the year, the Society employs part-time non-member carpenters to provide extra labour at peak periods. These people are paid on the basis of the amount of work they do whereas members themselves receive a flat salary of $100 a month each.

All the members play a role in preparing estimates, although the one Committee Member with technical education is most involved in this work. They calculate prices based on the cost of wood and other materials, an estimate of the amount of labour time and a 12% profit margin; they also have to add on a 25% Government sales tax and any other additional expenses which may be involved. Small-scale individual carpenters are able to quote lower prices, since they can evade the 25% sales tax and may be happy with little or no profit, and the Society is willing to lower its prices when necessary in order to obtain business. Similarly, when they know that competition for a tender is going to be very fierce, they are willing to lower their prices accordingly.

Ever since it started the Society has grown at an average of nearly 10% per year; they started with $1,200 in cash and their own hand tools which were worth about $4,000 altogether; by the end of 1983 there was a total of about $160,000 invested in the business. The members have earned a reasonable living in the meantime, as well as giving employment to large numbers of part-time workers, and in 1978 each member received a dividend of $60 and in 1980 a dividend of $500. In 1981 and 1982, by agreement of the members, no dividend was paid. They were saving money for a new co-operative shop which they proposed to open, and this new activity was duly started during 1982.

Because of their small numbers, most of the members play some part in the day to day management of the business. The Committee consists of the Chairman, the Secretary and three other members, and although they are all carpenters they are also the ones who are most concerned with the actual management of the enterprise. They are not resting on their laurels; they believe that their new shop is going to be successful but they are now planning to acquire a vehicle since they frequently experience problems in transporting both

The Stadi Furniture Co-operative Society Limited
Profit and Loss Account for the Year ending 31 December 1982

	Furniture	Shop	Total
	$	$	$
Sales	98,000	26,000	124,000
Cost of Sales	67,000	25,000	92,000
Gross Surplus	31,000	1,000	32,000
Wages, Rent, Depreciation and other Expenses			31,000
Net Surplus			$ 1,000

The Stadi Furniture Co-operative Society Limited
Balance Sheet as at 31 December 1982

Assets	$	$	Liabilities	$
Cash and Bank Balance		3,100	Accounts Payable	4,700
Accounts Recievable		300	Loan from SIDO	4,900
Stocks		6,900	Accumulated Surplus	5,900
Machinery and Equipment			Members'	
Cost	14,000		Contribution	800
Less accumulated				
depreciation	8,000			
		6,000		
Total Assets		$16,300	Total Liabilities	$16,300

their raw materials and their finished products. They are planning to apply for a loan for this purpose, and are reasonably confident that because of their good record their application will be approved.

Commment

The Stadi Furniture Co-operative Society Limited is a very encouraging, and regrettably unusual, example of a successful workers' co-operative society. A number of factors appear to have contributed to the situation. The members all came from a similar level and they formed the Society as a result of genuine hardship, rather than because they were persuaded or encouraged to do so by Government or other outsiders.

The Society has remained small enough to enable all the members to be in close contact with management decisions, and there is some indication that one of them provides a degree of leadership which is essential for success. There is no evidence that the members have attempted to become involved in politics, or that local Government or politicians have attempted to capitalize on this successful expression of co-operative ideology. Although some of their initial business came partly as a result of their being a co-operative, their later success has been founded entirely on their good performance rather than on any special preference which might be granted to them as a co-operative enterprise.

They have made use of the assistance provided by the Small Industries Development Organization, but it is significant that this organization is not exclusively intended to assist co-operative enterprises; its programmes are available to private as well as community businesses, and this Society has been run in a thoroughly business-like way.

Perhaps because of their previous hardship, the members have been content with reasonable earnings and have in fact accumulated substantial capital, part of which they have invested in a totally new venture. The early results for the shop suggest that it is actually being heavily subsidized by the original furniture venture, but this may be merely because it is a new enterprise and has not yet reached an economic level of operation. The Society's success in furniture manufacture was based primarily on members' skill, dedication and previous experience in the same business. It may be that they would have been better advised to expand into an area with which they had more familiarity, rather than into general retailing, but it is to be hoped that they will be able to recruit or themselves acquire the necessary expertise to make as successful a venture out of their new shop as they have out of their original business.